Maryland Equine Law

A Legal Guide to Horse Ownership & Activities

Dick—

It has been my privilege to have worked with you at the University Club — and benefit from your mentoring and friendship. I continue to model my "best business practices" from what I learned from you!

With much gratitude & admiration —

Kathleen

Kathleen J.P. Tabor, Esquire
&
Jan I. Berlage, Esquire

MARYLAND
EQUINE LAW

A Legal Guide to Horse Ownership & Activities

Maryland Equine Law

A Legal Guide to Horse Ownership & Activities

©2011 Kathleen J.P. Tabor and Jan I. Berlage

Cover Photography by Jim McCleary
Jimagery Photography
www.jimageryphotography.com

Photos on pages 12 & 126 by Katie Johnson.
All other black and white photos by Jim McCleary.

Research: Tara K. Clarke, an attorney with the law firm of Gohn, Hankey &
Stichel, LLP in Baltimore, Maryland.

Proofreading: Tracey M. Collins, a paralegal with the law firm of Gohn, Hankey &
Stichel, LLP in Baltimore, Maryland.

Printed in the United States of America.

Library of Congress Control Number: 2011923962

ISBN: 978-0-615-45720-8

Go Dutch Publishing, LLC
www.godutchpublishing.com

Dedication

I owe a debt of gratitude to my parents, Bernie and Helen Parsons, for fostering my passion of horses, writing, and the law at an early age. A huge thank you to my husband, Tim, for indulging my horse hobby and supporting me in my law practice. To my children, Adam, Allison, and Alexander, I thank you for your patience and support during my time at law school. To my equestrian friends and clients, I have learned much from your personal experiences and am indebted to your collective wisdom. And to Jan Berlage, my friend, colleague, and collaborator, for without your encouragement this book might never have been written.

~ Kathleen J. P. Tabor

"To the thunder of hooves..."

~ Jan I. Berlage

Introduction

This book was written for those involved with horses in the State of Maryland, for those interested in becoming involved in the industry and for the legal practitioners interested in learning more about "equine law." We offer this to you for practical advice and legal guidance. It is intended as a very basic guide as to various legal issues involved in the owning of horses and the operation of equine-based businesses. You may find useful information from the entire book, or from select chapters. Whatever your particular needs are, we hope you find the information contained within of interest and value to you.

Equine activities in Maryland are comprised of an impressive group of business owners and individuals. Rich in history, fanfare, and pageantry, the equine industry in Maryland offers a vast array of breeds and disciplines, from the work mule and carriage horse to the pleasure and sport horse to the steeplechase and flat track racers.

In Maryland alone, the horse industry is a significant factor within the economic realm of the state. Agriculture ranks as the number one commodity in Maryland. The equine industry ranks third among the various sub-divisions of the agriculture industry. The vast majority of business operations are considered "small business" entities, not multi-million corporate horse operations as one may have imagined. And, unfortunately, too many of these businesses operate on "borrowed contract language," Internet-searched documents, or oral agreements. These practices are neither good for the business owner or for the participant/clientele of these businesses.

But not all equine activities are considered a business enterprise. There are many individuals who own a horse (or two or more) merely for the pleasure of owning a horse. Yet, sometimes, a well-meaning piece of advice from a family member or friend may entice the horse owner to "change" the aspect of ownership from pleasure to business. Understanding how the state and federal government (particularly the

Internal Revenue Service) scrutinize such activities and distinguishes hobby from business is important to anyone involved with horses.

For many horse lovers, thoughts of contracts and conflicts are often ignored until a genuine dispute arises. Unless the activity involves a professional horse sport (and then not always), most participants of equine-related activities have not signed a contract detailing the business relationship or methods of resolving disputes. Knowing who can assist you in these conflicts and learning what resources are available can go a long way to preventing unnecessary conflicts.

Issues of liability are prevalent in this high-risk activity. In an age of litigating every perceived "wrong," it is not enough to rely on handshakes and good faith promises in the business dealings of horses. It does not matter whether you are a professional horseperson or just someone who loves the animal and indulges your passion as a hobby. A casual approach to using, owning, and even observing as a fan, could find you defending yourself in a lawsuit.

Understanding the nuances of the industry and the parameters of the law will assist you in preserving your rights. Although no one single document or any one attorney can guarantee you won't one day face a dispute or a lawsuit, having the properly-worded documents and a clear understanding of them can help you sleep better at night.

Those involved with horses often find their activities are not confined to a small parameter. Crossing county lines, state lines, and international boundaries have a distinct impact on how one addresses concerns of liability. Even the most experienced horseperson would be wise to consult an attorney on the peculiarities of each new transaction or venture. A few dollars spent reviewing a contract can save you hundreds, even thousands, of dollars later in litigation.

Furthermore, maintaining a mutually-beneficial relationship between and among equestrians is important, as the "world of horses" is a small one. Especially with the wide-use of the Internet and ease of travel, most equestrians will, at some point in their life, develop either a business relationship or a friendship with someone other than a person within their immediate circle of friends and family. Establishing a clear understanding of each other's rights and responsibilities will enhance the current and ongoing dealings with one another. Equally important is preparing for disputes and how best to resolve those conflicts while preserving relationships.

More often than not, most individuals involved with horses do not seek legal advice until there is a conflict. The participant and professional, whether hobbyist or business operator, should become familiar with the legal responsibilities and obligations one has and how the law may determine any rights or liabilities when engaging in equine-related activities. It behooves those involved in these activities to seek legal advice before a conflict or dispute arises.

This book will not only address the issue of potential liabilities and disputes found in equine-related activities by reviewing and analyzing the finer points of Maryland law and regulation of the equine industry, but also cover some of the nuances unique to the horse industry. The content of this book is a guide for those interested in the Maryland equine industry. It does not constitute legal advice, nor should it be used as a substitute for a consultation with a qualified legal professional. We have endeavored to be as comprehensive in coverage as possible, but also realize it is not all inclusive.

For the legal practitioner, we have developed this book as a guide for deeper understanding of the exceptional and distinctive characteristics of the horse industry. For the horse professional or horse lover, we have attempted to provide answers to those questions you may have about the legal issues implicated when one involves oneself with that marvelous, unpredictable animal known as the horse. For the individual needing legal advice, knowing you have an attorney on your "team" who can talk-the-talk of horse will allow you to focus on your passion: your horse. We encourage you to seek out those who understand the nuances of the industry and to develop a strong relationship with your attorney.

Table of Contents

CHAPTER 1

Sources of Equine Law

"From an equine perspective, it is important to note that counties have their own rules and regulations that directly impact horse ownership and care."

There is a wonderful line in C.S. Lewis's *"The Lion, the Witch and the Wardrobe"* that Aslan, the lion king, utters to Lucy and Susan after the White Witch kills him and he is resurrected. As Aslan explains, he has outwitted the White Witch because *"Her knowledge goes back only to the dawn of Time. But if she could have looked . . . into . . . the darkness before Time dawned. . .¹ she would have known of a superior law that allowed for his rebirth."* We should learn from the White Witch's mistake and never forget that equine law is governed by multiple sources. One needs to know the law at the federal, state, county and municipal levels as well as any rules that may apply through membership in any equine related association, such as the American Quarter Horse Association ("AQHA"), Arabian Horse Association ("AHA"), American Paint Horse Association ("APHA"), etc. This section will provide a primer on the different sovereigns that oversee equine issues in Maryland as well as the different sources of rulemaking inside each of them.

Sovereigns with Jurisdiction over Equine Activities: The Federalist System Hierarchy

(1) Federal
While the U.S. Constitution does not directly refer to federalism, it does divide government power into national government power, state

government power, and powers prohibited to government. National government power can be described as enumerated, implied, and inherent. Enumerated powers are found in the first seventeen clauses of Article I, Section 8 of the United States Constitution. Implied powers come from the "necessary and proper" clause, the last clause of Article I, Section 8. Inherent powers arise from the fact that governments have an inherent right to ensure their own survival. Under the supremacy clause of the U.S. Constitution, Article VI, Paragraph 2, federal laws are superior to all conflicting state and local laws.

Federal law generally plays a limited role in day-to-day of equine affairs that take place exclusively within Maryland. As is discussed in chapter 10, one of the most important areas of federal law related to equine activities is in the realm of taxation.

(2) State

Government at the state level in Maryland is conducted in accordance with the Maryland Constitution. Maryland, like the other 49 state governments, has exclusive authority over matters that lie entirely within the state's borders, except as limited by the U.S. Constitution. Almost all equine activities in Maryland will be governed to some extent by state law.

(3) County

At the local level, Maryland is notable among U.S. states for having a relatively small number of local governments. The primary form of local government occurs at the county level. Unlike most northeastern states, where county governments are weak administrative divisions with little authority, Maryland's 23 counties have substantial authority for governing within their borders. There are three forms of county government available to the state's counties. Note that the municipal government of Baltimore City, while not formally a county government, is typically considered to be on par with them.

(a) Commissioner Counties

County commissioners were first authorized in 1827 and commissioner counties do not have constitutional home rule power.

That is, they may not legislate on local matters without the prior specific consent of the General Assembly and in those areas where they do have authority it is narrowly construed. As a result of this, the General Assembly spends considerable time dealing with local issues, ordinances, and expenditures. The Maryland Constitution adopted in 1867 kept the power to pass public local laws vested in the General Assembly, which gave a lot of control over county government to county delegations in the General Assembly.

There are 16 counties in Maryland run by county commissioners. They are: Allegany, Calvert, Caroline, Carroll, Cecil, Charles, Dorchester, Frederick, Garrett, Kent, Queen Anne's, St. Mary's, Somerset, Talbot, Washington, and Worcester Counties.

(b) Charter Counties

Due partly to the large amount of time spent by the state legislature on local matters, the Maryland Constitution was amended in 1915 to allow counties the option of operating under a charter form of government. To adopt this form of government, the voters of the county must approve the charter which their charter board drafts. Once ratified, this gives the county control over almost all local matters, though power to regulate elections and to license and regulate the manufacture and sale of alcoholic beverages is reserved to the General Assembly. Some counties which operate under charters have a county executive while others vest executive functions along with legislative functions in the county council.

There are eight counties and the City of Baltimore that operate under the charter form of state government. They are: Anne Arundel, Baltimore, Harford, Howard, Montgomery, Prince George's, Talbot, and Wicomico Counties along with Baltimore City.

(c) Code Home Rule Counties

Due to the reluctance of many counties to adopt a charter form of government, despite wanting a measure of home rule, the Maryland Constitution was again amended in 1966 to create the code county status. If two thirds of a county's commissioners adopt a resolution that the county become a code county and a majority of the voters approve of the resolution, the county becomes a code county. In a code county the commissioners have home-rule powers and may enact legislation in the areas of the "express powers" of the charter counties, except there is no elected council or charter. In addition, the commissioners retain all the powers they previously had as a commissioner county There are five counties in Maryland that operate as code counties: Allegany, Caroline, Kent, Queen Anne's, and Worcester Counties.

From an equine prospective, it is important to note that counties have their own rules and regulations that directly impact horse ownership and care. Many times, since they target a small geographic area, these rules and regulations are much more detailed than those at the federal and state levels. It is a wise idea to contact your local county government about obtaining copies of the rules and regulations that directly impact horse ownership and care within its borders.

(4) Municipal Governments

Municipal Governments, or municipalities as they are commonly called, are towns or cities that are self-governing. Most commonly, they have been incorporated by an act of the Maryland General Assembly, though sometimes by referendum. There are 157 incorporated cities in Maryland, including Baltimore City.

From an equine prospective, it is important to note that, like counties, most municipalities have their own rules and regulations that directly impact horse ownership and care. If you are dealing with a municipality, you should contact it about obtaining copies of its rules and regulations related to horse ownership and care.

(5) Rules and Regulations of Horse Governing Associations

Besides the government entities that have authority over you and your horse, many equestrians are members of horse related organizations, such as AQHA, AHA, etc. Many times membership in these organizations is conditioned on a member's compliance with the organizations bylaws, rules, and regulations. This is especially true when it comes to issues of breeding or competition.

Different Sources of Law:
Statutes, Regulations, Ordinances and Common Law

(1) Statutes

So far, we have examined the sovereigns with jurisdiction over equine-related activities. We will now examine the different sources of law that may apply. The most common type of law is statutory, which means that it is a rule written by the legislature at the federal or state level. Statutes by their nature tend to be broad. They are usually elaborated on either by administrative agencies or courts.

(2) Regulations

Administrative agencies elaborate on statutes by drafting regulations to further define them. Administrative agencies adopt, amend and repeal regulations under the authority granted to them by either constitutional provisions or statutes. Unless the legislature has created an exemption, agencies must follow the procedures in the Administrative Procedure Act when adopting, amending or repealing regulations. Federal agency regulations are found in the Code of Federal Regulations, also known as the CFR. Maryland agency regulations are found in the Code of Maryland Regulations also known as COMAR.

(3) Common Law

In rendering their decisions, courts often further define the meaning of statutes through their rulings. This process is known as the Common Law. When there is no authoritative statement of the law, judges have the authority and duty to make law by creating precedent or "common law." Thereafter, the new decision becomes precedent, and binds future courts at the same or lower level under the principle of stare decisis, which is the policy of courts to stand by the precedent of earlier decisions and not disturb settled points of law.

(a) Federal Court System

But all case law is not the same. The judicial system is hierarchical. In the federals system, the general hierarchy is as follows:

U.S. Supreme Court

U.S. Court of Appeals

U.S. District Court (Trial Court)

The U.S. Supreme Court is the highest court in the land and governs all states. In federal cases, Maryland falls under the jurisdiction of the U.S. Court of Appeals for the Fourth Circuit. The Fourth Circuit also has jurisdiction over Virginia, West Virginia, North Carolina and South Carolina. It is headquartered in Richmond, Virginia. While states can have more than one U.S. District Court within their boundaries, Maryland has only one U.S. District Court with a Northern (Baltimore) and Southern (Greenbelt) divisions. It should also be noted that there are specialty courts in the federal systems, such as tax and bankruptcy courts.

(b) Maryland State Court System

In the Maryland state system, the hierarchy is as follows:

> U.S. Supreme Court
> Maryland Court of Appeals
> Maryland Court of Special Appeals
> Maryland Circuit Court
> Maryland District Court

The United States Supreme Court has jurisdiction over the Maryland Court of Appeals to the extent any case it hears implicates federal law or the U.S. Constitution. As to matters involving exclusively internal state issues, the Maryland Court of Appeals has the final word. Maryland Circuit and District Courts are trial level courts. Maryland Circuit Court is a trial court of general jurisdiction, whereas the District Courts jurisdiction is limited to smaller matters as described by statute.

(4) Ordinances

An ordinance is a local law. Although the method of enacting an ordinance will vary from county-to-county or municipality-to-municipality, they are generally passed by a legislative body and signed by a county or city executive and subsequently enforced by local police and district attorneys. County and Municipality laws are published in local codes.

Transactions Across State Lines

Transactions across state lines can present complicated questions as to where a case should be tried (venue and jurisdiction) as well as what law should apply (choice of law).

(1) Jurisdiction and Venue

Many times a lawsuit extending across state borders can be brought in multiple jurisdictions where there is either some nexus between the parties or where the injury arose. For a defendant to be hauled into court in a particular jurisdiction, that defendant must have minimum contacts with the forum state. Thus, for a court to have jurisdiction in a case, the plaintiff must show that the defendant has sufficient contacts, ties or relations with the state to justify personal jurisdiction over him or her. There are two aspects to this text. One, the state jurisdiction provisions must allow for jurisdiction and, two, the exercise of such jurisdiction must satisfy the due process clause of the Fourteenth Amendment to the U.S. Constitution. Because Maryland's long arm statute, Md. Cts. & Jud. Proc. Code Ann. § 6-103, is designed to extend the scope of jurisdiction to the limits of the Fourteenth Amendment's Due Process Clause, inquiry in Maryland on this issue depends on the Due Process Clause.

Under the Fourteenth Amendment, a defendant is subject to a court's jurisdiction if he or she has sufficient minimum and purposeful contacts with the state. Due process further requires the defendant's conduct and connection with Maryland be of a character that he or she could have reasonably anticipated being hauled into court there. In addition, the Court's exercise of personal jurisdiction over the defendant must not offend "traditional notions of fair play and substantial justice."[2] In applying this standard, courts look to the "quality and quantity of the potential defendant's contacts with the forum."[3]

In a case where the matter in controversy exceeds $75,000 and the parties are from different states, either party may elect to have the matter heard in federal court under the federal court's diversity jurisdiction.[4]

(2) Choice of Law

The second issue that must be confronted in cases involving transactions across state lines is which state's law should be applied. There are elaborate rules that govern this issue. The simple way around these rules, at least where a contract exists, is for the parties to expressly state which jurisdiction's law they wish to be applied. Short of such a choice of law provision, Maryland courts will apply the following rules:

(a) Contract

Absent a choice-of-law provision in a contract, Maryland courts apply the rule of lex loci contractus to matters regarding the validity and interpretation of contract provisions. "Under this principle, the law of the jurisdiction where the contract was made controls its validity and construction."[5] For choice-of-law purposes, a contract is made where the last act necessary to make the contract binding occurs.[6]

(b) Tort

Maryland adheres to lex loci delicti principles for all tort claims, i.e., Maryland courts apply the law of the place where the tort or wrong was committed. Under those principles, the place where the last event required to give rise to the tort occurred determines the law that should apply, and that in personal injury claims, the last event required to give rise to the tort is the injury.[7]

(c) Federal Courts Sitting in Diversity Jurisdiction

In a diversity case, a United States District Court sitting in Maryland applies Maryland's choice of law rule. This principle has been settled since *Klaxon Co. v. Stentor Electric Mfg. Co.*, 313 U.S. 487 (1941), which extended the rule of *Erie R.R. v. Tompkins*, 304 U.S. 64 (1938), to choice of law questions.

CHAPTER 2

Title and Ownership

"Whether a horse is obtained through a breeding, sale, auction, adoption, gift, or transfer, it is imperative that a paper-trail of ownership be established to help prevent any misunderstandings later on"

In Maryland, as in most states, a horse is considered "goods[1];" livestock that is either personal property or a business asset. This may be disconcerting for the horse owner who considers his/her horse a part of the family, but in reality, it is simply property. And as property, the horse owner should take adequate precautions when purchasing, selling, leasing, or using the horse as they would with owning a motor vehicle or other piece of property. So what does it mean to own a horse? What are the legal responsibilities of ownership? What documentation proves ownership?

Whether a horse is utilized for personal use or for business purposes, the owner should understand the basic liability of owning a horse, and take precautions to protect their right of title. Throughout this book, specific issues of personal and premise liability, animal health, taxes, sporting and use activities, and contract protection will provide guidance to those who own horses, wish to own horses, or to the legal practitioner assisting them.

To begin with, how does one prove that a horse belongs to a specific individual, such that the person caring for the horse is not merely a "keeper" but an "owner?" And how do these distinctions impact the management of the horse? Unlike an automobile, the State does not issue a title of ownership for livestock. The responsibility of establishing ownership is in the hands of the individual.

Horses primarily are identified by their specific use or purpose: racing or non-racing. The racing industry (Thoroughbreds, Standardbreds,

Arabians, and Quarter Horses) has very specific documentation for proving title (i.e. rightful ownership) and strict guidelines regarding documentation. All other breeds are too often exchanged on a handshake and an oral agreement. This method, not surprisingly, may result in disappointment and disputes.

A Sales and Purchase Agreement is merely the first step in establishing an exchange of ownership of a horse. The horse owner offers for sale to a potential buyer the opportunity to purchase the animal. After negotiation, the sale terms and conditions are made in writing via a sales and purchase agreement. After the sale is completed, a "Bill of Sale" is issued to the new owner (See Sample Forms).

The Bill of Sale is the "sales receipt" acknowledging the purchase of the horse. It documents the date of purchase, the amount paid, a description of the horse, details any warranties made by the seller and offers acknowledgements of the buyer (such as accepting the horse "as is" and "with all faults" with or without the professional examination of a veterinarian).

Additionally, some horses are "registered" with a breed association or equine organization such as the "American Quarter Horse Association" or the "United States Equestrian Federation." These registrations are required by the specific organization for the purpose of allowing the identified horse and/or owner/rider the opportunity to compete in equestrian shows, events, and competitions. The registration does not necessarily define who rightfully owns the horse. The registration details the recordation of the horse (by an individual - the purported owner) pursuant to the particular rules and regulations of that group or organization. Except for The Jockey Club or the U.S. Trotting Association, registration papers may not adequately identify the current owner particularly if a transfer of ownership was not completed or a minor child's name has been registered as the "owner" of the horse.

Whether a horse is obtained through a breeding, sale, auction, adoption, gift, or transfer, it is imperative that a paper-trail of ownership be established to prevent any misunderstandings later on. When multiple owners of a horse are involved, it may be advisable to consider filing a UCC Financing Statement establishing the secured interest in all or part of the horse (when "choice of law" is an issue, the perfection state determines perfection). Partnership and syndicate agreements also are methods of establishing percentage of ownership in a horse.

Because a horse is considered "personal property" it can be conveyed to a new owner through estate planning as well as purchase agreements. Although the horse is not recognized as a pet, it is possible to establish a "pet trust" for the care of your horse upon your death. Maryland is fortunate to have equine attorneys knowledgeable in estate planning and we strongly advise that you seek out these individuals for assistance.

Establishing the rightful owner of a horse goes further than who has the right to ride or use the horse. Ownership responsibilities beyond the basic care of the horse include liability issues, spread of communicable diseases, and carcass disposal. One particular problem arises when a horse is "free leased" to another individual and there has been no memorialization of the terms and conditions of the agreement. A clearly written document detailing who retains title and who is responsible for the care of the horse while under the custody of another will resolve many disputes down the road when the "new owner" wants to be able to sell or dispose of the horse without control from the titled owner.

CHAPTER 3

Equine Health

*"When you have the care, custody and control of a horse,
you must know which health regulations affect your
activities with the horse."*

Whether you own or lease a horse or if you are contracted to care for a horse, it is your responsibility to know those health regulations which affect the activities of the horse. Regulation at the federal, state, county and municipal level will vary dependant on the particular use of the horse. In the State of Maryland there are state-wide regulations affecting live and dead animals, commercial treatment (auction markets), showing, interstate transportation, and disaster or infectious disease guidelines. International import and export guidelines are federal based. Reporting cases of abused horses is managed at a county and municipality level. International movement of horses falls under the auspices of the federal government, as well as certain horse welfare regulations.

Basically, anyone who has the care, custody and control of a horse must provide minimum standards of care. Maryland law requires (1) nutritious food in sufficient quantity, (2) necessary veterinary care, (3) proper drink, (4) air, (5) space, and (6) shelter or protection from the weather.[1] However, each county has the authority to interpret the state regulation and impose its own criteria to meet these standards. Such criteria may include specific acreage ("space") per horse, or the use or prohibition of natural ponds or streams on the property ("proper drink"). The variations are too vast to include in one chapter, but a review of the County Code will assist you in complying with your county's specific regulations.

Federal Considerations

At the federal level, horses are regulated by the United States Department of Agriculture – Animal and Plant Health Inspection

Services (USDA – APHIS). The local Veterinary Service Area Office in Maryland is located in Annapolis.[2] Through this office, the USDA-APHIS issues health certificate endorsements and export certifications, conducts import inspections, responds to animal health emergencies, and provides a variety of educational programs. Although the United States has few requirements for exporting horses, the regulations governing the horse's importation into a specific country will vary. Information on those regulations can be found through the USDA-APHIS website (http://www.aphis.usda.gov/regulations/vs/iregs/animals/).

APHIS also takes an active role in the protection of horses from soring - a technique of irritating a horse's forelegs through chemical or physical means in order to produce a high-stepping (exaggerated) gait. The Horse Protection Act (HPA)[3] prohibits this practice, as well as the transportation of horses to and from competitive shows and exhibitions. Criminal and/or civil penalties can be brought against violators.

Infectious disease control and reporting of outbreaks also filters through the USDA-APHIS department. Reports and updates on diseases such as contagious equine metritis, an infection of particular concern to breeding operations, can be found at http://www.aphis.usda.gov/animal_health/index.shtml.

The Maryland Horse Industry Board

Created in 1998 by the General Assembly, the Maryland Horse Industry Board (MHIB)[4] operates through the Department of Agriculture. It is managed through an executive director and by a board of directors appointed by the Governor and represents various aspects of the horse industry. Inspectors of commercial horse stables and operations assist the MHIB in its mission to regulate the health and welfare of horses. These inspectors also are employed by the Veterinary Board to inspect vet clinics and veterinarian practices. Equine facilities that board five or more horses per year for compensation, or use one or more horses per year for lessons or hire, or sells five or more horses per year, are required to obtain an annual license through MHIB.

Issuance of a license results from a satisfactory inspection of the facility. Inspectors help direct operators on improving deficiencies in order to ensure compliance with the equine health standards of Maryland.

Maryland Horse Health Requirements

Health requirements for horses can be found in the Code of Maryland Regulations (COMAR) under Title 15, Department of Agriculture, Subtitle 11, Animal Health. Health certificates and a negative Coggins test[5] for horses, mules, and asses aged (9) months or older must accompany the animal when imported to the State of Maryland.[6] Equines traveling into Maryland for shows, exhibits, or other competitions must provide proof of a negative Coggins test.[7] Violators of these regulations are guilty of a misdemeanor and are subject to fines and/or imprisonment as provided for by law.[8]

For individuals exhibiting horses at a multi-livestock show, the State requires, along with a negative Coggins test, an Interstate Health Certificate (CVI). Since 2009, a "Self-Certification of Equine Health" form is required for all horses entering multi-livestock shows or exhibits. However, "(T)hose participating in equine only shows and events are exempt from this requirement."[9]

For organizers of these events, the Department requires notification sixty (60) days prior to the event, but will allow exceptions for those events sponsored, sanctioned, or otherwise approved by an association, coalition, or other entity which serves as an umbrella organization for multiple livestock exhibitions in a calendar year.[10] Although current regulations do not require organizers to collect CVIs, Self-Certification Equine Health Forms, or Coggins verification, it is considered a good business practice and encouraged by the Department of Agriculture as well.

Humane treatment of horses at auction markets also falls under the auspices of the Maryland Department of Agriculture.[11] Humane treatment is defined as "treating livestock in a manner that avoids unnecessary suffering or pain; and providing livestock, when necessary, with adequate feed, water, veterinary care, and shelter."[12] Individuals or companies who transport horses to or from an auction are also regulated, particularly if a "downer"[13] is involved.[14] The Department of Maryland has implemented policy guidelines regulating auction market operators and haulers. A copy of the policy can be obtained by contacting the State Veterinarian's office in Annapolis at (410) 841-5810. Additional regulations for the general transportation of horses were passed by the General Assembly in 2007 which require specifications of trailers used to haul horses and impose a civil fine of $500 for the first offense, and $1,000 for the second and subsequent offenses.[15]

Several regulations relevant to infected animals or disposal of a domestic animal that has died of a contagious or infectious disease require specific action by the individual, often including reporting requirements.[16] Violators of any equine health regulation can face fines and/or imprisonment. In 2007, the General Assembly added administrative penalties in a fine amount of up to $10,000 that could be assessed instead of, or in addition to, any other penalty allowed by law for violations that include, but not limited to, falsifying health certificates, failing to comply with quarantines, failing to prevent or control communicable diseases, refusing access to premises for inspections, selling or improperly disposing of the carcass of a diseased animal, or failure to comply with any regulation.[17]

Abuse Regulations

In Maryland, there are many subtle, county-to-county variations in local interpretation of cruelty, neglect and abuse standards. (See "Appendix One," page 185) for a contact list for Animal Control authorities for the City of Baltimore or County.) However, the State of Maryland also has a general law prohibiting a person from overdriving or overloading an animal, depriving an animal of necessary sustenance, inflicting unnecessary suffering or pain on the animal, or failing to provide the animal with sufficient food, water, shelter, protection from the weather and veterinary care.[18] Penalties for this misdemeanor may include fines and/or imprisonment and may also require the violator to participate in and pay for psychological counseling.

Overall, if you are in possession of a horse, you are responsible for its health and welfare. Your veterinarian, local extension services, MHIB, and equine associations, such as the Maryland Horse Council or American Horse Council, can provide you with the necessary information to assist you in complying with all the federal, state, and local regulations for your particular situation.

CHAPTER 4

Tort Law

*"A Maryland animal owner may be held liable for damages
or injuries caused by its animal either under a
strict liability or a negligence standard."*

As Alexander Pope observed, "To err is human, to forgive, devine."
But this avoids the fundamental question of who should bare the
cost of the mistake. Tort law is our legal system's answer to this question.
Since horse owners are not immune to error, it is important that they,
as well as their attorneys, understand the intersection between tort and
equine law. This chapter is designed to provide such an understanding.

Negligence

We generally think of claims for personal injury or property damage
caused by another in terms of negligence and take for granted that one
must be at fault to be held responsible for another's injury. But this is
not always the case. As we will discuss, in certain situations, one may be
held strictly liable and parties can usually contract around negligence
principles. Still, negligence remains the primary way in which costs
associated with accidents are allocated among parties.

Negligence is "any conduct, except conduct recklessly disregardful
of an interest of others, which falls below the standard established by
law for protection of others against unreasonable risk of harm."[1] It
does not exist apart from the facts and circumstances upon which it is
predicated.[2]

In order to establish a cause of action for negligence, the plaintiffs
must prove the following elements: (1) that the defendant was under a
duty to protect the plaintiff from injury, (2) that the defendant breached

that duty, (3) that the plaintiff suffered actual injury or loss, and (4) that the loss or injury proximately resulted from the defendant's breach of the duty.[3] Let's briefly examine each of the elements:

(1) Duty of Care

The first, and arguably most important, element to a negligence claim is whether the defendant owed the plaintiff a "duty of care." [4] It has often been said, "There can be no negligence where there is no duty that is due; for negligence is the breach of some duty that one person owes to another."[5]

But how is it determined that such a duty exists? "It is for the court to determine, as a matter of law, what characteristics must be present for a relationship to give rise to a duty... It is for the jury to determine whether facts in evidence establish the elements of that relationship."[6] Courts consider, among other things:

(1) The foreseeability of harm to the plaintiff;

(2) The degree of certainty that the plaintiff suffered the injury;

(3) The closeness of the connection between the defendant's conduct and the injury suffered;

(4) The moral blame attached to the defendant's conduct:;

(5) The policy of preventing future harm;

(6) The extent of the burden to the defendant and consequences to the community of imposing a duty to exercise care with resulting liability for breach; and

(7) The availability, cost and prevalence of insurance for
the risk involved.

Equestrians generally owe a duty of "ordinary" or "reasonable" care
to keep people safe from their horse-related activities.[7] This duty will
take on different forms depending on the relationship between parties,
as discussed later in this chapter.

(2) Breach of Duty

The second element of a negligence claim is that of "breach."
Simply put, the inquiry is whether the defendant failed to meet its
duty of care to the plaintiff. This is usually a factual question left to the
trier-of-fact.

(3) Injury

In contrast to intentional torts, nominal damages will not support
a negligence claim. The plaintiff must show actual damages.

(4) Causation

The causation element of a negligence claim requires the plaintiff
to prove that there is a reasonable connection between the defendant's
negligence and the plaintiff's damages.[8] This is known as proximate
cause. For example, in a case where a defendant allowed a rope to hang
in a loop very low across a public street, the defendant was negligent,
and that negligence was held to be the proximate, though not the
immediate, cause, of the plaintiff's injury, which was caused when the
plaintiff's horse was frightened when a stranger moved the rope.[9] As
the court explained:

[T]he defendant is liable where the intervening causes, acts,
or conditions were set in motion by his earlier negligence, or
naturally induced by such wrongful act, or omission, or even
it is generally held, if the intervening acts or conditions were
of a nature, the happening of which was reasonably to have
been anticipated, though they have been acts of the plaintiff
himself.[10]

Proximate cause is also sometimes viewed as "causation in fact." It requires a direct relationship between the negligent act and the injury.[11] This concept is also discussed as "but for" causation, since a plaintiff must show that his or her injury would not have occurred "but for" defendant's negligence.[12]

Defenses to Negligence Claims

Besides the claim that one has done nothing wrong, one of the more obvious defenses to a negligence claim is that the injured party was responsible, in full or in part, for his or her own injury. This is a particularly strong defense in Maryland, which continues to subscribe to the common law theory of contributory negligence. Under this regime, any negligence on the part of the injured acts as an absolute bar to recovery.[13] To put this in context, most other states have abandoned contributory negligence in favor of comparative negligence. While the exact mechanism in which it applied vary, in a comparative negligence system, the injured party may still recover some of his or her damages even if partially to blame for causing the accident, although the recovery is usually reduced by the percentage the plaintiff was at fault.

There are exceptions to contributory negligence in Maryland. One such exception exists when a defendant violates a statute. In certain circumstances, such as a violation of a statute may "place the entire responsibility for such harm as had occured upon the defendant. Another exception is known as the "last clear chance doctrine." Under this doctrine, a negligent plaintiff 'place[s] the entire responsibility for such harm as has occurred upon the defendant.'"[14]

Maryland also adheres to the common law exception to contributory negligence known as the "last clear chance doctrine." Under this doctrine, a negligent plaintiff can recover if he or she is able to show that the defendant had the last opportunity to avoid the accident or, put another way, that the plaintiff can show the defendant's negligence and the existence of "something new or independent" occurred after the plaintiff's negligent act.[15] The underlying rationale for this exception is to mitigate the harshness of the contributory negligence rule. The defendant can also use this doctrine as a defense. If the plaintiff has the last clear chance to avoid the accident, the defendant will not be liable.

Strict Liability

"Under Maryland law, the owner of a domestic animal may be liable under two separate theories of liability for injuries caused by his animal-strict liability or negligence."[16] "Strict liability" is where a defendant is held liable for his or actions regardless of fault. The doctrine covers four primary areas: (1) Product liability; (2) Abnormally dangerous conditions; (3) Mislabeled goods; and (4) Dangerous animals. While one can envision situations involving equestrian activities where one of the first three areas might be at issue, the last area is obviously of particular significance to horse owners.

In Maryland, "[i]n order to hold an animal owner strictly liable for injuries caused by his animal, a plaintiff must demonstrate the owner knew or, with reasonable care, should have known that the animal had a propensity to commit the particular type of mischief that was the cause of harm."[17] Liability may also extend to a landlord who is boarding a dangerous horse, if the landlord has control over the stable where the horse is boarded so that the landlord has a duty to inspect those premises.[18]

In sum, if you are a landlord with horses on your property, you want to use care in who you allow to board horses on their property and horses that those people bring to you. If reasons dictate, that a dangerous horse be on your property, you must make sure nothing goes wrong as you will be held strictly liable if it does.

CHAPTER 5

Professional Malpractice

*"In a malpractice case against veterinarian, you will need
to engage an expert, normally another veterinarian,
to testify that the applicable standard of care in
that case was breached by the defendant."*

Professional malpractice is a species of negligence law. It differs from general negligence in that professionals are held to a higher standard than other people in their chosen profession. Whether the professional is a doctor, accountant, lawyer, or most commonly in the context of equine law a veterinarian, he or she will be held to that degree of care and skill which a reasonably competent professional engaged in a similar practice would use.[1]

Malpractice Standards

To establish a cause of action for professional malpractice, a horse owner must prove the existence of four elements: (1) a duty owed to the horse owner; (2) a breach of that duty by the defendant; (3) that the breach was the actual and proximate cause of the horse's injury; and (4) damages.[2] Again, the primary difference between a professional malpractice claim and that of mere negligence is the standard of care element. It is the plaintiff's burden to show that standard of care was breached.[3]

Veterinarian Malpractice Claims

One group of professionals equestrians most rely upon is veterinarians. As with many types of professionals, veterinarians are required to be licensed in Maryland and are governed by Agriculture Article of the Maryland Code.[4] There are relatively few reported court decisions in Maryland concerning veterinarian malpractice. This is most likely attributable to the cost of litigating such a claim and the limited damages a successful plaintiff can hope to receive in such a case. Another reason may be that the patients of veterinarian's are unable to complain, many times causing claims to go unreported.

1. The Need and Expense of Expert Testimony

Malpractice litigation is expensive because it requires expert testimony as to the standard of care in a particular profession. In a malpractice case against veterinarian, the plaintiff will need to engage an expert, normally another veterinarian, to testify that the applicable standard of care in that case was breached by the defendant. Many times veterinarians (as with other professionals) will be reluctant to testify against their colleagues. This also may help to limit the number of veterinarian malpractice claims are filed. That being said, if the case warrants it, with a little research one should be able to find a veterinarian who will testify and lawyers who practice in this area will usually know or know of those individuals.

2. Limited Damages

For most horse owners, their horses are like a member of the family. The law, however, has traditionally viewed horses as mere personal property.[5] Under this paradigm, horse and other pet owners' damages are limited to the market value of their pet. Emotional distress damages simply are not available.

In Maryland, damages compensable for losses incurred to a pet are limited by statute. In contrast to the traditional rule, Maryland allows a pet owner to be compensated for damages that exceed the market value of pet, but such damages, along with the loss of the pet itself, are capped. The applicable statute is MD Code, Court & Judicial Proceedings § 11-110, which states:

> § 11-110. Pet injuries; damages
> (a) (1) In this section the following words have the meanings indicated.
> (2) "Compensatory damages" means:
> (i) In the case of the death of a pet, the fair market value of the pet before death and the reasonable and necessary cost of veterinary care; and

(ii)   In the case of an injury to a pet, the reasonable and necessary cost of veterinary care.

(3)   (i) "Pet" means a domesticated animal.
        (ii) "Pet" does not include livestock.
(b) (1) A person who tortiously causes an injury to or death of a pet while acting individually or through an animal under the person's direction or control is liable to the owner of the pet for compensatory damages.
(2)   The damages awarded under paragraph (1) of this subsection may not exceed $7,500.

Arguably, equine do not fall within this so-called "Pet Statute." By its terms, the statute is limited to "Pets" and expressly excludes "Livestock" from being "Pets." Elsewhere in the Maryland Code, the term "Livestock" is defined as "living or dead...equine, unless otherwise provided.[6] The fact that horses may not qualify as pets for purposes of the Pet Statute does not mean a horse owner can recover emotional distress damages for the loss of a horse - horses are still merely chattel in the eyes of the law and one cannot normally recover emotional distress damages for the loss of property, no matter how dear that property may be to that person. But, arguably, it does eliminate the cap on damages incurred by way of veterinarian bills. This makes sense in light of the market value of some horses, which would certainly justify making expenditures, (in excess of $7,500), to try and save them. The famous racehorse Barbaro, who received a fatal injury during the Preakness Stakes at the Pimlico Race Course on May 20, 2006, is a case in point.

It should also be noted that, while the law presently treats pets as chattel and does not allow for their loss to give rise to emotional distress damages in most jurisdictions, the law is constantly changing and there is considerable pressure by pet owners, animal rights groups and other to change the law in this arena.[7]

Statute of Limitations

A veterinarian malpractice claim is not governed by the statute of limitations for medical malpractice claims, which only applies to Health

Care Providers as defined by MD Code, Court & Judicial Proceedings § 3-2A-01, i.e., those providing health care services to human beings. Thus, veterinarian malpractice claims should be governed by the same statute as other negligence claims, so that a horse owner has three years from the date a cause of action "accrues" within which to file his or her claim.[8] The discovery rule, which suspends accrual of the statute of limitations until the plaintiff discovers the wrong should apply in this context.[9]

As a practical matter, however, if you suspect that your veterinarian may have committed malpractice, you should immediately seek a second opinion by a respected veterinarian. This may include getting X-rays, blood work and tissues samples in certain circumstances. This is not just a legal issue; it is the right thing to do by your horse, especially when remedial measures may still be possible. But it also makes sense in terms of documenting your malpractice claim, since it is easier to garner evidence of malpractice when it has just occurred rather than later on.

Malpractice Alternatives

There are other options available to pursuing a veterinarian who one believes has committed malpractice that can be pursued in addition, or as alternative, to filing a professional malpractice lawsuit. These options include:

1. Maryland State Board of Veterinary Medical Examiners. The state administrative board that oversees the practice of veterinarian medicine in Maryland is known as the Maryland Board of Veterinary Medical Examiners (BVME). It is the job of the BVME to investigate claims filed against veterinarians who practice in this state. One can file a complaint with the BVME by going on its website, which can be found at www.mda.state.md.us/animal_health/vetboard. A copy of a BVME complaint also can be found in the "Forms" section of this book. If the BVME finds that your claim has merit, it can bring disciplinary action against the veterinarian, including suspending or revoking his or her license to practice veterinarian medicine in this state.

2. Better Business Bureau. Many veterinarians are members of the Better Business Bureau or other professional organizations, which will investigate complaints filed against their members and take disciplinary action where appropriate. The Better Business Bureaus of Greater Maryland's website, which includes information on filing a complaint, can be found at www.baltimore.bbb.org.

3. Website Review. There are many websites which allow you to rate veterinarians and other professionals anonymously. Two such websites are www.vetratingz.com and www.citysearch.com.

4. Newspapers and Other Media Outlets. In the right circumstances, where a veterinarian's malpractice may rise to the level of public interest, you may be able to get the media to investigate the veterinarian's practice or tell your story. Obviously, if you are going to take this approach, you must be careful not to violate any slander or libel laws. One of the safer ways of doing this is by filing a lawsuit for which there is a qualified immunity and then letting the media know.

5. Other Legal Grounds. Because of the costs a professional malpractice claim entails, due to the need to hire an expert witness, one may want to consider filing suit on other grounds in addition, or as an alternative, to filing a malpractice claim. For instance, one may have a breach of contract claim if the veterinarian did not fulfill his or her promises. A straight negligence claim also may be able to be maintained, especially if the veterinarian or a member of his or her staff failed to comply with any statute or regulations governing their care of your horse.

Before you take any of these actions, however, you should make sure that there is no other way to resolve your problem and that the veterinarian has in fact committed malpractice. Most veterinarians are extremely capable professionals and a valuable resource to the equine community. The suggestions above are intended only for the very few who should not be practicing veterinary medicine.

Other Types of Professional Malpractice

While this chapter has focused primarily on veterinarian malpractice, it bears repeating that a professional malpractice claim can be brought against any professional in the horse industry in which a higher standard of care may apply. Thus, farriers, trainers, massage therapists, and other professionals who work with horses may be the targets of such claims. If you fall into one of these categories, you should take extra care in reviewing the suggestions given in the previous chapter on how to immunize yourself from potential tort liability.

CHAPTER 6

Contracts

"The best contract is one that is customized by an attorney familiar with the business practices of the horse industry and the client's particular needs."

Although legal advice is available to horse owners and businesses, most individuals involved with horses do not seek legal advice until there is a conflict. For many horse lovers, thoughts of contracts and conflicts are often ignored until a genuine dispute arises. Unless the activity involves a professional horse sport, most participants of equine-related activities have not signed a contract detailing the business relationship or methods of resolving disputes. Aside from signing the occasional "liability contract" for the use of a horse for riding, most individuals never sign a contract for riding lessons or the care or training of their horse.

The many possible participants involved in equine-related transactions may include owners of horses, owners of barns or training centers, lessees of horses, volunteers, independent contractors, and employees, horse trainers and instructors, as well as myriad other professionals and equine-related service providers (e.g. farriers and health-care providers). For the most part, those involved with horses consider one another "friends" or, at the very minimum, on friendly terms with one another. The "hand-shake deal," a common practice for most horse-related transactions, can become a source of bitter legal disputes which can destroy the continued business (and personal) relationships among the participants. Many equestrians often consider an oral understanding as sufficient in creating a contractual relationship, relying on the faith that those involved will do what's right and on the hope that nothing serious will occur. It is true that Maryland recognizes oral contracts, but consider what happens once a conflict arises. Often it becomes a matter of who tells a more credible story ("he said / she said") without sufficient written documentation to support one's version over another. It is all too true that an oral contract is only as good as the paper it's written on. It is important to note that conflicts that may arise when there is no written contract can easily be resolved with a basic written contract.

A written contract provides an opportunity for both parties to clearly state their understanding of each other's rights and responsibilities. There is nothing inexpensive when it comes to being involved with horses. Taking the time to put the agreement to paper, and paying for an attorney who is familiar with equine activities to review the contract, often will save much more expense (and heart-ache) later on. By far, the best method to address potential conflicts and disputes is to put the terms of the relationship in writing. "The value of a valid, enforceable contract is that it allows the parties to avoid surprise in the event a business transaction does not go as planned."[1] All parties to any transaction will benefit from a well-drafted document.

The basic elements to a contract requires two (or more) parties who have the capacity to enter into an agreement (i.e. minors cannot enter into a legal contract) and valid consideration exchanged between the parties (i.e. payment from one party for the service of another party). Furthermore, the object and purpose of the agreement must be one that is legal (one cannot contract to perform an illegal act). The terms and conditions of the agreement must be mutually understood and accepted by both parties (i.e. "a meeting of the minds"). An agreed method for resolving breaches to the contract (other than going directly to litigation) also should be included among the various terms and conditions of the contract. Particularly with equine contracts, alternative dispute resolution will assist in preserving ongoing business and personal relationships in the small world of equine activities.

Additionally, there are certain contract formalities that will affect particular contracts. For instance, in Maryland, under the Statute of Frauds, "a contract for the sale of goods for the price of $500 or more is not enforceable by way of action or defense unless there is some writing sufficient to indicate that a contract for sale has been made between the parties and signed by the party against whom enforcement is sought or by his authorized agent or broker."[2]

The Parol Evidence Rule also is applicable to written contracts. This rule ensures that the contract signed is the complete and entire agreement between the parties. Although oral or other written understandings may have been the basis of creating the final agreement, these "outside" agreements do not alter the final outcome if their terms and conditions were not incorporated into the final contract.

Maryland's Commercial Law code has numerous applications to contracts relevant to the equine industry. A particularly important provision in the Code is the Lien on Livestock. [3] The livestock lien enables the owner or operator of a "livery stable or other establishment" who has provided care or custody to a horse, the right to assert a lien against the horse's owner for failure to pay board, care, training, veterinarian and farrier services, and other maintenance services for the horse. A well-written boarding or training agreement should include a provision noting this right of lien.

The components to any well-drafted equine contract will depend largely on the type of agreement and for which purpose (or purposes) the agreement is being made. Consider the numerous types of transactions: employment, services bartering, equipment, land and horse leases, recreational and sporting events, facility use, participant and hold harmless agreements, breeding and stallion management, show and racing, sale and lease, boarding, training, and lessons. Knowing if and when provisions of the Uniform Commercial Code, Maryland Commercial Code, parol evidence, and other contractual requirements are needed will ensure both parties a fair and equitable agreement. Consulting with your attorney prior to drafting or signing will help you understand the terms and conditions of your contract and any consequences for breaches.

Most importantly, get **EVERYTHING** in writing. A mere handshake in today's litigious world may ultimately result in exorbitant legal expenses and ill-will among good friends (See Sample Forms).

CHAPTER 7

Premises Liability

"You should walk your property on a regular basis, checking for, among other things, holes that horses might trip on, bad fencing, and faulty equipment."

Equine owners hold a special appreciation for land. Among other things, a certain amount of land is necessary to keep and board horses. Whether an individual owns their own land or rents, they should be familiar with potential liability that can arise from ownership or control of it. This area of the law is known as premises liability. Premises liability is a species of negligence law that addresses the duty of care a landowner or one who controls such property owes third-parties who venture onto their premises. Like with other areas of negligence law, the lynch pin is "duty of care." The duty of care an owner or occupier of land owes to visitors varies depending on the entrant's legal status.[1] That status will normally be one of the following:

(1) Invitee;

(2) Social guest;

(3) Licensee; or

(4) Trespasser.

We will discuss each of these in turn.

Before we do so, it should be noted that, "mere ownership of land or buildings does not render the owner liable for injuries sustained by tenants or invitees rightfully on the premises, for the owner is not an insurer of such persons but owes them the duty only to exercise ordinary care to render the premises reasonably safe."[2] It is also well settled that, "when the owner has parted with his control, the tenant has the burden of the proper keeping of the premises, in the absence of an agreement to the contrary; and for any nuisance created by the tenant the landlord is not responsible."[3]

But there is an exception to this rule. A stable owner who leases a portion of his property to horse tenants and reserves another portion of the property for the common use of the tenants must exercise ordinary care to keep the common area reasonably safe.[4] "[L]andlord liability in common areas is generally premised on the control a landlord maintains over the common areas. This duty stems in part "from the responsibility engendered in the Landlord by his having extended an invitation, express or implied, to use the portion of the property retained by him."[5] The stable owner's duty to exercise reasonable care to keep common areas safe extends not only to his or her tenants but also to his or her tenants' guests.[6]

What this means for equine boarding facilities is, if you rent your land to someone who holds dominion over it, you should not be held responsible for their carelessness. As a practical matter, however, if someone is injured on your property, you may still be sued. Thus, it is in your interest to keep a watchful eye on your tenants to make sure their horse operations are being conducted in a safe and reasonable manner. You will also want to be aware who is coming on your property and why as this will control what duty is owed to these entrants.

Invitee

The highest duty a stable owner can owe to third-party on his or her property is that of invitee. The term "invitee" really means "business invitee," since such person is defined as "a person on the property for a purpose related to the possessor's business."[7] An owner owes such a person a duty to "use reasonable and ordinary care to keep the premises safe for the invitee and to protect the invitee from injury caused by an unreasonable risk which the invitee, by exercising ordinary care for the invitee's own safety will not discover."[8] In other words, an invitee is owed a duty of ordinary care by the owner to keep the property safe.[9]

Invitee status can be established under one of two doctrines: (1) the mutual benefit or (2) implied invitation.[10] Under the mutual benefit theory, the invitee generally enters a business establishment for the purpose of purchasing goods or services.[11] This theory places great weight upon the entrant's subjective intent, and inquires into whether the entrant intended to benefit the landowner in some manner.[12] For example, boarders at an equine facility will be deemed invitees because the owner of the facility is benefitting financially from the boarders' use of his or her land. Likewise, it has been held that those who pay money to train their horses at racetracks are business invitees.[13]

In comparison, the implied invitation theory is objective and does not rely on any mutual benefit.[14] Rather, the circumstances control, such as custom, habitual acquiescence of the owner, the apparent holding out of the premises for a particular use by the public, or the general arrangement or design of the premises.[15] The gist of the implied invitation theory is the distinction between mere passive acquiescence by an owner or occupier in certain use of his land by others and direct or implied inducement.[16] Additionally, to be considered an invitee under this theory, it is necessary that:

> [T]he person injured did not act merely on motives of his own ... but that he entered the premises because he was led by the acts or conduct of the owner or occupier to believe that the premises were intended to be used in the manner in which he used them, and that such use was not only acquiesced in, but was in accordance with the intention or design for which the way or place was adapted and prepared or allowed to be used.[17]

A person can lose invitee status if he or she remains on the premises beyond a reasonable time after the invitation has expired.[18] Moreover, a business owner is not an insurer of the safety of its invitees. It is not required, for example, to take precautions against a sudden attack from a third-party until he or she knows or has no reason to know that the invitee is endangered.[19] This standard applies to those who board their horses and otherwise pay to use an equine facility.[20]

Social Guest

A social guest, sometimes referred to as a licensee by invitation, is not an invitee in a legal sense, since he or she is invited on the premises for reasons other than the owner's business. A stable owner owes such a person a "duty to exercise reasonable care to warn ... of dangerous conditions that are known to the possessor but not easily discoverable."[21] This standard would apply to those who are invited onto the stable owner's premises but do not pay to be there.

Licensee

A bare licensee is one who enters the property of another with the possessor's knowledge and consent, but for the licensee's own purpose or interest.[22] Such a person is owed by the property owner a duty to refrain from willfully or wantonly injuring him "and from creating 'new and undisclosed sources of danger without warning [him or her]."[23] Put another way, an equine facility owes no duty of care to the licensee, except to avoid willful or wanton misconduct towards him or her.[24] An example of a licensee would be a farrier, veterinarian or other professional who ventures onto the premises to service the horses on the property.

Trespasser

A trespasser is one who intentionally and without consent or privilege enters another's property."[25] He or she is owed the most limited duty: to refrain from willfully or wantonly injuring or entrapping.[26] A stable owner owes such a person no duty of care to exercise reasonable care in maintaining his or her land in a safe condition.[27]

Fireman's Rule for Fire Fighters and Police Officers

Maryland has long recognized in the context of premises liability what is know as the "Fireman's Rule." This name is somewhat of a misnomer, since the rule covers both firefighters and police officers. In certain circumstances, the rule operates to bar firefighters and police officers from tort recovery for injuries sustained in the course of their employment.[28] The Fireman's Rule establishes the status of firefighter and police officers to be that that of a licensee only, not that of an invitee.

The Fireman's Rule is best explained in terms of public policy, and not by application of the law of premises liability. As the Maryland Court of Appeals explained in *Flowers v. Rock Creek Terrace*, the rationale behind the rule is as follows:

> [I]t is the nature of the firefighting occupation that limits a fireman's ability to recover in tort for work-related injuries. Instead of continuing to use a rationale based on the law of premises liability, we hold that, as a matter of public policy, firemen and police officers generally cannot recover for injuries attributable to the negligence that requires their assistance. This public policy is based on a relationship between firemen and policemen and the public that calls on these safety officers specifically to confront certain hazards on behalf of the public. A fireman or police officer may not recover if injured by the negligently created risk that was the very reason for his presence on the scene in his occupational capacity. Someone who negligently creates the need for a public safety officer will not be liable to a fireman or policeman for injuries caused by this negligence.[29]

Thus, property owners or occupiers of land, under normal circumstances, owe no duty of reasonable care to firefighters and police officers.

This rule may not apply to other public officials, who may be deemed invitees, depending on their positions and reasons for being on particular premises.[30] It may not even apply to firefighters and police officers when their injury has not been caused by the risk that occasioned his or her presence at the property. For example, in *Tucker v. Shoemake*, the Maryland Court of Appeals applied this same analysis to hold that the Fireman's Rule did not preclude tort recovery by a police officer who was injured when he fell into a manhole as he was walking through the common area of a trailer park on the way to responding to a domestic dispute call from one of the trailer park residents. The Court explained that because the police officer's injuries had not been caused by the risk that had occasioned his presence at the trailer park, the Fireman's Rule was inapplicable.[31]

Limiting the Risk of Premises Liability

Since it is a form of negligence law, the same tips provided in Chapter 4 with respect to minimizing potential tort liability also apply to premises liability. Three of these tips are especially helpful in the case of premises liability. First, you should always endeavor to create a safe environment for people and horses. If you see something is broken or creating a dangerous condition, you should fix it right away. Don't leave this to chance. You should walk your property on a regular basis, checking for, among other things, holes that horses might trip on, bad fencing, and faulty equipment.

Second, some dangerous situations are unavoidable. In such situations where you may not necessarily be able to fix or eliminate the hazardous condition, do the next best thing – warn of its existence. This is especially true if you have people on your property that may not be as familiar with horses as you. For instance, even the best behaved horses do unexpected things and those who have been around horses know to take caution when walking behind them. While this may seem obvious to you, it may not be obvious to someone else. In simply explaining the hazard of walking behind a horse, you may prevent someone from being kicked. Finally, if you know you are going to have people on your property and it is reasonable to do so, it is always a good an idea to get a waiver of liability from them.

CHAPTER 8

Liability Issues and Insurance

*"When it comes to protecting your assets you will either
purchase insurance or be "self insured.""*

When dealing with horses, the question of insuring a horse (or equine business) is often asked. Depending on your particular role with the horse (owner, lessor, professional, or business facility) or how you are using your horse, the age of the horse, and the potential of the horse will determine what type, if any, of insurance coverage you would consider purchasing.

Liability Issues

Keep in mind that there is an inherent risk to the use and sporting of horses and the State of Maryland recognizes the assumption of risk (voluntary and aware). Individuals who participate in horse related activities assume those risks with no right to a claim of damages arising from one of those inherent risks, particularly if they have contributed to their own injury. Furthermore, as you may recall from Chapter 4, Maryland uses a contributory negligence standard in determining damages (as opposed to "comparative" negligence). Under the theory of contributory negligence, if an individual has any responsibility for their own injuries, then they receive nothing. Maryland is one of the few remaining states using contributory negligence. But even with contributory negligence on their side, no one would be excused for actions resulting from an act of gross (willful and knowing) negligence. Such would be the case if an equine professional allowed worn tack to be used on a horse or if the professional placed an inexperienced rider on a horse requiring a more skilled and experienced rider.

As with any negligence standard, there are elements to each case that must be analyzed in determining whether or not an individual is entitled to recovery. The elements of duty of care, breach of duty, causation, and harm/damages must exist for a cause of action in negligence to be exist.

There must first be a duty of care. This means that the equine professional or service provider (owner/operator) must have a specific relationship with the individual that has been injured (such as a student or customer). Second, there must be a breach of this duty. Determining this element is both subjective and objective. Was something done by the equine operator that resulted in the injury? Was the action reasonable under the circumstances or could the injury been foreseen? Was the breach caused by a person who held themselves out as a professional or one with extraordinary knowledge? If so, this individual would be held to a higher standard of care than the average person. Was the breach the cause of the injury? Was there some other reason for the injury to occur (such as the rider professed to have extensive knowledge in riding, but in reality, had not ridden a horse consistently in many years)? And finally, was there harm done from the breach? Is the injury a direct result of the failure of care, the breach, and the cause? If any one of these elements is missing, then there can be no recovery.

In addition to the assumption of risk and contributory negligent standard, the Maryland "Recreation Act" provides immunity from liability when an activity involves educational and recreational purposes and there is no collection of money. Therefore, there is no duty of care to the participant by the operator of the event. An example of this would be the land-owner who permits riders to use the trails in their woodlands, or cross their fields while chasing fox (provided the landowner has not charged anyone for the particular use of the land), or permitted pony rides for a charity event. Again, it is important to consult with your attorney before assuming your particular activities are covered under the Maryland "Recreation Act."

Given these "safeguards" to equine businesses (and to private owners), it has not been necessary for Maryland to enact an "equine liability statute." Many states have enacted one version or another of this statute. However, it is important that the equestrian understand the limitation of these statutes. Equine activity liability laws are statutes enacted to provide some form of immunity from liability for equine-activity service providers. They are designed to reduce lawsuits. Language typically found in such laws releases an equine-activity service provider of responsibility resulting in an injury or death of a participant in equine activities unless the equine-activity service provider has failed to exercise due care. The language and level of protection will vary from state-to-state and there are no universal definitions of "equine professionals," leaving the question of what happens to nonprofessionals. Additionally, strict compliance (including placement of signs, font size, specific use of language, etc.) by the service provider is required, or the immunity is nullified.

In general, Maryland courts will enforce written releases and waiver of liability forms. A written notice to riders, students, or customers as to the inherent risks of equine activities is an asset to the service provider. And, again, written releases negate the need for an equine liability law. However, it is important when using a liability release, that an attorney familiar with equine activities reviews the document. It is equally important not to "borrow" the language from a form found on the Internet, another facility's form, or cut and paste from canned documents. Particularly due to the fact that Maryland uses the contributory negligence standard and has other general protections in place, the language found in most equine liability releases is not beneficial to Maryland activities.

Insurance

To assist in liability protection, one must consider the particular equine activities in which you are engaged, what your relationship is with these activities and third parties, and how best to protect your assets (including your horse). In reality, you either purchase insurance or you "self-insure" your activities and assets. Self-insuring would require disciplining yourself to dedicate a separate savings account for those times when liability may be at issue. Determining how much to set aside is subjective at best. Consulting with your attorney or your accountant may help you determine how much you may need to set aside (or what type of insurance coverage to purchase).

If a horse is owned and used for personal reasons only, typically the homeowners' insurance policy will include a rider for liability coverage. This would be similar to any accident a visitor to your home may have (slip and fall) or if your horse was to damage someone else's property (such as a fence). You would want to discuss with your insurance agent if your current policy covers personal-use horses. There also are separate "horse owner liability" policies available.

However, if the horse is leased to a third-party or used in the course of a business transaction (such as giving lessons), then the homeowner's policy will not cover the potential liability. This is when you would obtain liability coverage through commercial or business liability insurance. The application will ask in detail how many horses are to be covered, how the horses are used (boarded, shows, lessons, etc.) and where the horses are used. It's recommended that you seek quotes from two or three different insurance agencies as you will find not every agency will cover all aspects of horsemanship (i.e. trail riding, carriage driving).

Other business insurance issues to consider would be worker's compensation and professional liability (particularly if you are a trainer or instructor). For special events that are not regularly part of your business operations, such as a party or horse and pony show, you may be able to obtain a "special events" liability policy. This is a temporary or one-time use policy for a specific occasion or period. This liability policy is particularly helpful to small organization's that do not carry a policy of general liability.

If your business is a non-profit organization you also may want to consider D&O (directors and officers) insurance to protect key members of a company's management team from lawsuits brought about due to their job-related activities. Errors and Omissions insurance coverage concerns performance failure and negligence with respect to your company's products and services (not the performance and duties of management). A sit-down with your attorney or insurance agent to review the specific operations of your business will help you determine what type of policies and how much coverage is deemed necessary to protect your assets.

In general, Maryland insurance coverage and costs are currently about equal to similar states. But it is still important to check around to get the best rate possible for your particular needs. A list of the various types of equine insurance can be found in "Appendix Two" (page 191).

CHAPTER 9

Land Use

*"Agriculture ranks as the #1 industry in the State of
Maryland. The "equine industry" is ranked
third within the agricultural industry.
Horses and land are important commodities."*

For those individuals involved with horses, the primary land use concerns will center on premise liability, property damage, bodily injury, and zoning standards and restrictions. Throughout this book we have attempted to address the intricacies of those issues involving property damage and bodily injury (torts) as well as premise liability and insurance issues. Risk assessment is the very first step the horse owner or horse-business owner needs to take in protecting their assets. Owning a horse or operating an equestrian business will involve the use of land, whether it's owned, leased, or used for a one time event or activity. It's crucial that the property owner assess all of the risks and benefits involved in equine activity use.

Attractive Nuisance Doctrine

A brief reminder that, (as discussed in Chapter 7) in Maryland, "for purposes of premises liability, distinction exists between trespassers and others."[1] It also is important to distinguish Maryland from some of our neighboring states who recognize the doctrine of "attractive nuisance." The doctrine of attractive nuisance is recognized in some states, not in Maryland, and it places the responsibility of safeguarding one's property of a "dangerous thing or condition that will foreseeably lure children to trespass."[2] In Maryland, "(W)hile required to provide ordinary care for invitee, owners of real and personal property owe no duty to a trespasser, even though the trespasser is a child of tender age, except to abstain from willfully or wantonly injuring or entrapping such person."[3]

In Maryland, a landowner's liability to any trespasser (child or adult) is the same. There is no greater liability to the landowner if the trespasser is a child. See *State v. Baltimore Fidelty Warehouse Co.*, 176 Md. 341 (1939) for the case authority regarding the rejection of the attractive nuisance doctrine in Maryland.

Maryland Recreation Act

Often times, in Maryland, a landowner of vast acreage may be asked permission from those wishing to cross their land for recreational purposes, such as for a trail ride or a fox chase, or to use the property for a charitable event like a 4-H or a pony club show. Such activity may be a one-time use or a seasonal request. For those property owners who permit this activity on their land and who do not collect a fee for its use, the State of Maryland created immunity from liability through a statute generally referred to as the "Maryland Recreation Act."[4] The immunity from liability only applies, however, if the activity is for an educational and/or recreational purpose and no collection of money is made.[5]

"The Maryland recreational statute provides landowners good liability protection and a review of case law has found few, if any, judgments to support the (above) belief" that anyone entering property covered under the statute who is injured can sue and win a judgment.[6]

Waiver of Liability

Should a property owner desire to use their land for more profitable means, then a liability waiver is strongly advised. However, in using a waiver, it is best to avoid "canned" or "borrowed" documents and to obtain legal counsel for drafting a customized waiver for the particular use or business operation. When drafting a waiver, use clear and concise language, and avoid ambiguous terms and excessive "legalese." This agreement is not between lawyers, but between lay persons who must clearly understand what responsibilities each party has and what rights they may be relinquishing.

A waiver should detail the inherent risks of the particular activity, specify the duration of the waiver, and include an indemnification clause. Distinguish between adult and minor participants - minors cannot contract, and therefore, cannot waive their rights. However, having the parent or guardian sign the waiver does give notice to the adult of the risks of injury, or even death, involved in the activity.

It also is recommended that along with customary contract language, that alternative dispute resolution methods be incorporated into the waiver, along with acknowledgments, authorization and assertions relevant to the participant's health, experience, skills, rules, safety and emergency treatment.

When asked to sign a liability waiver (also known as a "hold harmless agreement") it is imperative that as the participant, you read the entire agreement before signing. Ask for clarification if any term or meaning is unclear to you. Understand what risks you are assuming and that you have a voluntary choice to accept or reject this particular activity and its risks. It is important to note that every individual is held only to that standard of which an individual of like intelligence and age would be capable of appreciating and accepting such risks. Therefore, the more one partakes in a particular activity, the higher of a degree of appreciation and understanding of the risks. As an example, a 22-year old person riding a horse for the first time would not be held to the same standard as a 22-year old individual who has been schooled and working with horses since the age of five. The bottom-line with waivers and equine activities: know what you are getting involved with and understand the hazards and potential risks you undertake by participating in that activity.

Equine Liability Statutes

There is a very good reason why Maryland has not enacted a catch-all statute for limiting liability for equine professionals and businesses. The first compelling reason is the protection afforded those operating equine activities through the contributory negligence standard. Considering the fact that Maryland utilizes the contributory negligence standard, with the assumption of risk doctrine, the Maryland "Recreation Act," and the common law of contracting (validating the use of waivers of liability), it makes little sense to layer on an additional regulation that at best gives a false sense of protection to equine professionals, handlers, or businesses.

True, many (if not most) states have enacted one form or another of an equine liability law. States that have enacted equine liability statutes have done so to reduce lawsuits due to accidents caused by the inherent nature (i.e. unpredictability) of horses. Language typically found in such laws releases an equine-activity service provider of responsibility resulting in an injury or death of a participant in an equine activity unless the equine-service provider has failed to exercise due care. The language and level of liability protection will vary from state-to-state. "Equine Liability Acts often refer to 'equine professionals,' leaving the question of what happens to nonprofessionals."[7] And, "(G)iven the broad directives concerning immunity, the statues appear to offer significant relief from liability; however, this relief may be illusory, since the statutes also contain exceptions that markedly limit the grants of statutory immunity."[8] Specific exceptions granting immunity of liability under the equine-liability laws include intentional torts, negligence, willful disregard and trespass violations (as well as the professional sport of horse racing).

These statutes merely direct the equine-activity service provider to give notification of the inherent risks being assumed by the participants. In some states, utilizing equine liability statutes, if this language is not clearly posted (including specific letter sizing on signs) or included in a written contract, the equine service provider cannot rely on the statutory provisions for protection against liability in the event of a lawsuit. Equine-service providers should consider the importance of obtaining "preventative legal medicine" ranging from complying with state regulations and obtaining adequate insurance, to drafting detailed contracts appropriate to the specific circumstances of their transactions.[9]

At best, an equine liability statute is another form of notice to those participating in equine activities and the assumption of those inherent risks. At worst, it's another layer of bureaucracy requiring absolute compliance or forfeiting all benefit of immunity. An equine liability law, as well as any waiver of liability, will never exempt one from liability due to gross negligent acts.

Land Protection Mechanisms

Maryland provides a variety of methods to protect the encroachment of residential and commercial development on existing tracts of land primarily used for agricultural purposes (horse operations are considered agricultural throughout most of the state). But as with most regulations in Maryland, there are nuances from county-to-county in the regulation language. The most recent "Right to Farm" movement has found its way into all twenty-three counties in Maryland. Finding the regulation will vary; it may be found in the County Codes under "agriculture" or "farming" or "health" or "zoning" – you may have to do some in-depth research to find the specific regulation. However, the essence of the regulation is to preserve as much open space for farmland as possible. It provides guidelines for farmers and non-farm residents for sharing the limited resources available to all citizens. These regulations recognize the economical value of farming and the need to preserve this activity.[10]

Agricultural protection zoning, also found in the County and Municipal Codes, typically benefits commercial farming. The regulation helps keep large tracts of land relatively free from non-farm development. These specific zones are areas designated where farming is the desired land use.

Cluster zoning also acts as a method of preserving open space and creating transitional areas between farms and residential areas. Residential homes are grouped together on smaller lots to protect the open land. Parcels not developed may be protected by a conservation easement. This zoning method typically is not designed to support commercial agriculture.

A conservation easement is essentially a deed restriction allowing landowners to protect their agricultural property from development. The Maryland Environmental Trust[11] was created by the General Assembly in 1967 to preserve land. This tool allows the landowner to protect scenic open spaces, which is very beneficial to the recreational use of horses. This method affords farms protection against development and also offers several tax advantages associated with the donation of the easement; federal and state income tax credits, property tax credits, and inheritance taxes. If the trust organization approves the easement, it is a great method of passing land to the owner's children without paying huge estate taxes, provided the Trust grants the easement. The easement is perpetual and runs with the land, which permits the landowner to sell the land (although the property value may be reduced due to the easement) while protecting the property from undesirable development or sub-dividing.

The Maryland Agricultural Land Preservation Foundation[12] was established by the General Assembly in 1977 and is part of the Department of Agriculture. As part of its mission, the Foundation strives to protect agricultural land and woodland as open space. Again, this is advantageous to equine-related activities such as trail riding or fox chases. It provides protection in two ways: through the designation of an agricultural district and through agricultural easements. Eligibility and procedural requirements may differ slightly depending on which method the landowner chooses to preserve the property.

Other Zoning and Licensing Issues

As a horse owner or owner of an equine business, you may be required to comply with particular codes and permits, depending on the particular county or municipality in which you reside. When developing or converting a parcel of land for equine habitation and/or activities it is your responsibility to know the particular zoning and permit requirements. Structures such as signage, barns, arenas, and outdoor lighting will require permitting and zoning approval. Will your particular operation have an impact on local traffic? How will manure be managed? Will it be stored, spread on fields, or removed? What are the environmental impacts on the number of horses on the property? Do you have the requisite license for your particular operation? Are you required to have a license if you aren't "commercial" but accept other horses to be boarded at your barn?

The basic rule of thumb with horses and land use is "be a good neighbor." Know your rights and responsibilities, make an honest assessment of your premises and capabilities, limit your liability as much as you can, and consult with a good equine attorney to review your operations.

CHAPTER 10

Taxes

"IRS regulations state that a series of profitable years is strong evidence that the taxpayer is engaging in the horse-related activity for profit."

Few things in life are certain, taxes are one of them. But there is good news for those involved in the equine industry – horse related activities offer many tax benefits. These tax advantages range from income tax deductions to charitable donations to agricultural classifications for property tax purposes. To fully take advantage of these opportunities and to stay out of trouble with taxing authorities, it is important to understand the often Byzantine web of federal, state, and county taxes. This chapter is not designed to offer tax advice but, rather, merely to provide a bird's eye view of these treacherous waters. To properly navigate these torrents, you should engage a professional accountant or attorney with a working knowledge of horses. This chapter will help you select the right professional and know what questions to ask him or her.

Record Keeping

Probably the most important thing involving taxes is not so much a legal issue as it is a record keeping one. In order to properly prepare your taxes, you need to keep thorough and complete records of your business activities. At the end of the year, you will need to add up all of the money your equine business brought in (revenue) and all of the money you spent on it (expenses). The difference between these two numbers is your business earnings for the year. If you earned more than you spent, you made a profit and will have to pay income taxes on it. If you had a loss, in certain circumstances, you may be able to deduct that loss from other income you earned for tax purposes. Either way, you will need to be able to show the Internal Revenue Service ("IRS") and the Maryland Comptroller the documents that support these figures; particularly if you donate a horse or equine equipment to a school, police department, therapeutic riding center or other non-profit organization and hope to take a charitable deduction. Remember the law, including tax law, is not so much about truth as it is proof. In short, it is essential to keep organized and accurate records of your equine activities for tax purposes.

Federal Income Taxes
Pit Falls for the Unwary: Hobby and Passive Loss Issues

Two problems commonly faced by equine business owners when audited by the IRS or Maryland Comptroller are the "hobby loss" and "passive loss" tax rules.

(1) Hobby Loss Provisions

Section 183 of the Internal Revenue Code ("IRC") provides that a taxpayer cannot deduct expenses of an activity which are greater than income from that activity if the activity is "not engaged in for profit." In other words, tax laws require that in order for a taxpayer to deduct expenses that exceed income, the taxpayer must demonstrate that he or she is engaged in a horse-related activity with the intention of producing a profit. Initially, the burden of proof falls upon the taxpayer. But, if a profit can be shown in two of seven consecutive years beginning with the first loss year, the burden shifts to the taxing authority to disprove the "general presumption of profit intent."

In determining whether an activity is engaged in for profit, all facts and circumstances with respect to the activity are taken into account. That having been said, the IRS cites nine factors that it is particularly interested in. They are as follows:

1. The manner in which the taxpayer carries on the activity.

In layman's term, the IRS wants to know that the taxpayer is conducting his or her equine related activity as a business. For example, is the taxpayer maintaining complete and accurate books and records, is the way in which that taxpayer carries on the activity in a manner substantially similar to others carried on for profit, is the taxpayer adopting new techniques to make the activity profitable, while abandoning those methods that are not work, etc.[1]

2. The expertise of the taxpayer or his/her advisors.

The IRS will look to see whether the taxpayer or someone engaged by the taxpayer is researching and studying the economics of the horse related activity to better the taxpayer's business. The lack of such effort is indicative that the taxpayer is engaging in the activity for reasons other than primarily profit. [2]

3. The time and effort expended by the taxpayer in carrying on the activity.

The more time and effort a taxpayer expends in the particular equine activity, the greater likelihood that his or her involvement in the horse-related activity is profit motivated.[3]

4. Expectation that the assets used in the activity appreciate in value.

IRS regulations specifically state that the term "profit" includes appreciation in the value of the assets, including land, used in the activity. Thus, even if no profit is derived from current operations, the taxpayer may argue that an overall profit may result from the appreciation of the land, horse, or other assets used by the business.[4]

5. The success of the taxpayer in other similar or dissimilar activities.

IRS regulations state that the fact that you have engaged in similar activities in the past and converted them from unprofitable to profitable enterprises may indicate that your present activities are profit motivated.[5]

6. The taxpayer's history of income or losses with respect to the activity.

IRS regulations state that a series of profitable years is strong evidence that the taxpayer is engaging in the horse-related activity for profit. A series of years in which a loss is sustained, however, does not necessarily imply the opposite. It is taken for granted, especially during the taxpayer's initial start-up period that he or she may not make a profit. If the losses continue over a sustained period of time, though, this will undercut the taxpayer's argument that the activity is being engaged in for profit.[6]

7. The amount of profits in relationship to losses and in relationship to the amount of the taxpayer's investment and the value of the assets used in the horse-related activity.

A critical factor that the IRS examines is whether the taxpayer's profit motive is the amount of profits he or she has obtained in relation to the amount of losses incurred over the period of operation. An occasional small profit from a horse-related activity which generates large losses, or from an activity in which the taxpayer has made a large investment, will not generally be determinative that the activity is a business. Conversely, a substantial profit, though only occasional, will generally be indicative that the equine-related activity is engaged for profit.[7]

8. The financial status of the taxpayer.

If the taxpayer lacks substantial income or capital from sources other than the horse operation, this favors finding the activity engaged in for profit. In contrast, if the taxpayer has substantial income from other sources, it is more likely that the activity will be viewed as a hobby, not engaged in for profit, especially if personal pleasure or recreational elements are involved.[8]

9. Elements of personal or recreational pleasure.

The more personal or recreational pleasure the taxpayer obtains from the activity the more likely the activity is not being engaged in for profit. But the fact that the taxpayer obtains a substantial amount of pleasure from engaging in the activity is not sufficient by itself to prove the activity is not engaged in for profit.[9]

Although the IRS regulations state that none of the above factors is necessarily more important than any other, court decisions in this area seem to place more weight on the first four factors.[10]

(2) Passive Loss Provisions

Under the 1986 Tax Reform Act, your ability to deduct losses is dependent on your active participation in the business. This means that, if you have a few horses someone else is managing, your losses may not be deductible. Active participation, however, does not require that you physically perform work on the farm or with your horse(s). If you are actively making decisions about what is happening with the business, you may be able to deduct your losses to offset your regular income, so long as such activity is "material."

Material participation is satisfied by establishing that the owner spends 500 or more hours actively participating in the business during any taxable year. If the owner does not meet the 500-hour test, he or she may qualify with 100 or more hours if he or she participates on a regular, continuous basis throughout the year and meets certain other criteria. Satisfying the requirements of this test, however, is more difficult than the 500-hour test. Hours spent by a husband and wife may be combined to accommodate these requirements. If an owner cannot prove material participations, losses can only be taken against other passive income.

"Ordinary and Necessary" Expenses

If a horse-related activity is being engaged in for profit, all "ordinary and necessary" expenses of the operation are deductible.[11] Most costs associated with breeding, raising, training, or showing horses other than capital expenditures are normally deductible.

Capital Expenditures

It is important to note that capital expenditures are generally not deductible as "ordinary and necessary expenses." Instead, these costs are spread over a number of years as depreciation or cost recovery deductions. The appropriate number of years is generally specified in the tax code with few exceptions.[12]

1.   Depreciation of Race Horses

Race horses may generally be depreciated over three to seven years. Longer periods of depreciation may be elected, and always apply in the case of foreign-based horses. Racehorses that are over two years old and breeding horses over twelve are depreciated over three years; all others are depreciated over seven years.

At first glance it seems more advantageous from a depreciation standpoint to purchase a horse over two years old. In the case of the IRS rules, note that age is determined by the actual date of birth, not the industry-accepted January 1 of each year. Furthermore, to prevent taxpayers from purchasing at the end of the year and obtaining a large depreciation deduction, if more than 40% of the purchases during one year are made during the last quarter, reduced depreciation results.

2. Depreciation of Farm and Other Equipment

The seven year period of depreciation used for most horses also applies to fencing and most farm machinery and equipment. Automobiles, light duty trucks, horse trailers and vans are normally depreciated over a five year period. Single purpose agricultural structures are written off over ten years, while barns, stables and other non-residential buildings are written off over 20 years.

State Taxes
Maryland Income Taxes

Maryland income taxes for the most part piggyback federal income taxes. In other words, Maryland uses a taxpayer's federal adjusted gross income with certain exceptions to determine a taxpayer's liability. Consequently, the rules that apply in the federal context to horse-related businesses more often than not also pertain to Maryland state income taxes.

Maryland Agricultural Land Preservation Program
Agricultural Easements

Horse Owners with their own farms may want to consider the tax benefits associated with putting such land into a conservation easement.

A conservation easement is an agreement whereby the landowner sells or donates certain development rights in real property to a governmental entity or legally recognized land trust (collectively, "Easement Holder") in exchange for income, estate and other property tax benefits, while maintaining ownership of the land. Such easements primarily preclude residential, commercial, or industrial development on the property, but are subject to individual negotiation. A conservation easement may be sold to an Easement Holder at its fair market value ("FMV"), at a reduced rate, or donated.

1. Sale of Easement

If a landowner sells a conservation easement to an Easement Holder for FMV, the proceeds from the sale of the easement may be subject to both federal and state capital gain taxes. Such a sale, however, may have estate tax benefits. By removing certain development rights, the value of the land will likely be reduced and, thus, heirs will not have to pay as much estate tax on the property.

2. Bargain Sale or Donation of Easement

If an easement is sold for less than its full easement value (a "Bargain Sale") or donated, the uncompensated value may be treated as a charitable contribution for federal and state income tax purposes. An independent appraiser hired by the landowner will determine if a charitable contribution has been created by the transaction and its value.

a. Federal Tax Benefits

Until December 31, 2009, the federal tax benefits of donating a conservation easement depended on the adjusted gross income and occupation of the landowner. If the value of the charitable contribution is 50% or less of the landowner's adjusted gross income, it may be entirely deducted in one year. If the value is greater, it may be spread over as much as 16 years. Qualified farmers and ranchers may deduct up to 100% of their income for up to 16 years.

b. Maryland State Tax Benefits

A landowner who donates a conservation easement may choose

to take a deduction on their State income tax, or they may choose to take an income tax credit. They may not take both. The credit is only available to individuals and single-member limited liability companies ("LLCs"), not to corporations, partnerships, or other business entities. Moreover, to qualify for the State income tax credit, the landowner's donation must have been made to either the Maryland Agricultural Land Preservation Foundation ("MALPF") or the Maryland Environment Trust ("MET"). The maximum State income credit is $5,000.00 per year. The remainder of the credit may be carried forward for up to 15 years for a maximum credit of $80,000.00. When multiple owners share a charitable donation of a conservation easement, each landowner is separately entitled to their proportionate share of the tax credit up to $5,000.00 per year. For instance, a husband and wife as owners of the conservation easement donated may, even if filing jointly, take up to a $10,000.00 credit per year as a couple.

c. Property Tax Credit

A landowner will pay no tax on land that is donated to the MET for fifteen years from the date of donation. At the end of that 15-year period, unimproved land subject to the donated easement will be assessed at the highest agricultural rate. This rate is currently $500.00 per acre. Property will qualify for this assessment rate even if the property is not actively farmed. If the property is in agricultural use, it will be assessed at the appropriate agricultural level. But the tax credit and assessment rate will not apply to any residential improvements, or to a minimum of one acre around these improvements.

d. County Property Tax Benefits

Approximately one-third of Maryland's counties offer property tax credits or other tax benefits for landowners donating conservation easements. To find out more about such programs, one should consult with the program administrator in the county in which the land to be donated is located.

Agricultural Assessment For Property Tax Purposes

Maryland law provides that lands which are actually devoted to farm or agricultural use shall be assessed according to that use. In 1960, Maryland became the first state to adopt an agricultural use assessment law in an effort to promote the conservation of farm land. The agricultural use assessment law and its corresponding programs are overseen by the Maryland Department of Assessments and Taxation ("SDAT"), which is responsible for assessing real property for tax purposes in Maryland.

The agricultural use assessment law encourages agricultural conservation by reducing the value of land to a value that correlates to its use for agricultural purposes as opposed for example to its value if it were developed. In almost all circumstances this will mean a lower assessment for property tax purposes. Even small farms, such as a ten-acre horse farm, can take advantage of this law.[13] It should be noted, however, that certain risks in the form of potential tax penalties can result from receiving the agricultural use assessment. Thus, a landowner should carefully evaluate the actual tax savings against those risks.

How Does One Calculate the Benefit of Such an Assessment?

To understand the benefits to such an assessment, one needs to understand that a property tax bill is the product of the assessment on the real property multiplied by the property tax rate. This is true for all property tax situations, regardless of whether or not the land receives the agricultural use assessment. Property tax rates are expressed as a certain number of dollars and cents per $100 of assessment. While some cities and towns in Maryland impose a separate property tax rate for property in that jurisdiction, for illustration purposes, we will only consider county and state property tax rates. We will use a typical county rate of $1.00 per $100 of assessment and state rate of $.132 per $100 of assessment resulting in a combined rate of $1.132. To determine what tax savings can be realized by receiving the agricultural use assessment, an examination of the level of assessment with and without the use assessment must be made. The actual value assigned to an acre of farmland averages about $300. Land that does not receive the agricultural use assessment will be assessed based on its market value.

Assume that a 100 acre parcel of land has a market value of $3,000 per acre. The total value of the parcel would be $300,000 (100 x $3,000). The same 100 acre parcel receiving the agricultural use assessment based on a value of $300 per acre would be $30,000 (100 x $300). The taxes using a combined tax rate of $1.132 per $100 of assessment would be $339 [($30,000 ÷ 100) x $1.132] under the agricultural use assessment and $3,396 [($300,000 ÷ 100) x $1.132] under the market value assessment – a difference of $3,057 or $30.57 per acre. While this shows the potential benefit one may receive from an agricultural use assessment, it should be noted that the tax savings decreases as the market value of the land decreases. For example, if the land is only worth $1,000 per acre rather than the $3,000, the total taxes for the 100 acres would be $1,132 [($100,000 ÷ 100) x $1.132] and the tax savings would be $793 or $7.93 per acre. The closer the market value comes to $300, the less the tax savings.[14]

What Property Qualifies?

It should be noted that agricultural assessments apply to the land, not to the property owner, and not all real property can qualify for such an assessment. The agricultural use assessment law directs SDAT to determine whether the land is "actively used" for farm or agricultural purposes and defines "actively used" as "land that is actually and primarily used for a continuing farm or agricultural use."

In other words, SDAT's sole focus is on the nature and extent of the use of the land. The primary test used by the Department is directly related to the phrase "actively used." While the Department has published formal regulations and procedures which are available to the public, they can be summarized as follows:

(a) What is the nature of the agricultural activity? Is the land tilled or is it in pasture or woodland, or a combination?

(b) Is the agricultural activity truly a bona fide agricultural activity that is generally recognized as such by the agricultural community?

(c) Is the agricultural activity the primary use of the land or does it appear that the primary use is non-agricultural?

(d) Is the agricultural use a continuing operation or only temporary in nature?

In most cases, there is little doubt as to whether a particular piece of property is being used for agricultural purposes. In situations, however, where it is unclear, another test known as the $2,500 gross income test is used. Under which, the property owner is required to certify that the agricultural activity on the property results in an average annual gross income of $2,500 or more. Once this certification is made and verified by SDAT, the agricultural use assessment will be granted.

Restrictions on Agricultural Use Assessments

Agricultural use assessment cannot be granted, regardless of the agricultural activity, to land used for a home site. This principle applies to tenant homes as well as the primary home. By state law, a home site is deemed to be one acre, unless obviously larger in size. Whatever the size, the home is valued and assessed at its market value as is all other non-agricultural land.

Another important restriction is land zoned for a more intensive use at the request of the owner or a person who had previously had an ownership interest in the land. If a rezoning occurs at the initiative of the county, the land may retain the agricultural use assessment. If the owner requests the rezoning, the use assessment must be removed. The law also prevents granting the use assessment to relatively small parcels of land. For example, no parcel under three acres in size is eligible, unless one of the following conditions are met:

(1) the land is owned by an owner of adjoining land that is receiving the farm or agricultural use assessment and the land is actively used (limited to only two parcels of less than 3 acres); or

(2) the owner receives at least 51% of the owner's gross income from the active use of the small parcel; or

(3) the parcel of less than 3 acres is part of a "family farm unit." This term means that the owner of a larger farm may separate out of the larger parcel not more than 1 smaller parcel for each immediate family member. These smaller parcels must remain in active agricultural use, they must be contiguous to the larger parcel, and they must be owned by the immediate family member.

The final restriction relates to subdivided parcels. That is, parcels of land included in a subdivision plat. Here, the property owner is allowed a maximum of five parcels that are less than 10 acres each. These parcels must meet the definition of "actively used." Any number of parcels in the subdivision plat over the maximum of vie which are under 10 acres in size will be assessed based on the market value.

The Potential Downside

One of the potential downsides to operating a horse farm assessed in the Agricultural Use category is that it may later be subject to an Agricultural Transfer Tax. The Agricultural Transfer Tax applies at the point of sale of land that receives the agricultural use assessment. Technically, the tax is imposed on the written instrument (deed) conveying title to the property and it must be paid before the document can be recorded in the land records of the county. The amount of tax is calculated by the assessment office and it is collected by the county finances office. State Law (Sections 13-301 through 13-308 of the Tax-Property Article) provides the statutory framework for the Agricultural Transfer Tax. Generally, the law specifies that the tax is due on all transfers of agricultural land unless the purchaser is willing to promise to keep the land in agricultural use for five full taxable years after the transfer. Then, the tax is waived by filing a Declaration of Intent with the county assessment office.

The law also provides stiff penalties for property owners who waive the tax by filing a Declaration of Intent and later fail to comply with the agreement. Here, it is important to note, the Declaration of Intent represents a promise to maintain the land as farm or woodland for five full consecutive taxable years. This document includes a statement that the purchaser agrees to meet the criteria necessary to receive the agricultural use assessment as it applies to farmland or woodland. Loss of the use assessment during the five year period will result in the tax, plus the penalty, being imposed.

CHAPTER 11

Employment Law

"IRS regulations provide detailed guidance for determining whether a person providing services to an individual is an employee or an independent contractor."

One of the highest costs a stable owner may have is that of having employees. Besides wages, employees mean more taxes, higher insurance and other costs associated with them. Many times, horse-related businesses will try to avoid these expenses by simply labeling their employees 'independent contractors.' But avoiding such costs is not as easy as switching labels. There are major differences between employees and independent contractors and the penalties associated with mislabeling them can be steep. As one legal commentator has observed, "Equine facilities usually learn this the hard way after they receive a challenge from the Internal Revenue Service (IRS), government agency, or a person is hurt on the property."[1] To help avoid this mistake, this chapter explores the differences between the two types of workers and the implications of each.

Federal Law

Federal law differentiates between workers who are employees and those that are independent contractors in certain situations. Generally, employees are afforded more protection than independent contractors. Many federal statutes utilize the common-law definition of "employee." This is because these statutes merely use the term "employee" without defining it and by doing this it is assumed Congress meant to describe the conventional master-servant relationship as understood by common-law agency doctrine.[2] So who does the common law consider an employee? According to the U.S. Supreme Court, to answer that question one must look at the following factors:

> In determining whether a hired party is an employee under the general common law of agency, we consider the hiring party's right to control the manner and means by which the product is accomplished. Among the other factors relevant to this inquiry are the skill required; the source of the instrumentalities and tools; the location of the work; the duration of the relationship between the parties; whether the hiring party has the right to assign additional projects to the hired party; the extent of the hired party's discretion over when and how long to work; the method of payment; the hired party's role in hiring and paying assistants; whether the work is part of the regular business of the hiring party; whether the hiring party is in business; the provision of employee benefits; and the tax treatment of the hired party.[3]

While no one of these factors is determinative, Maryland courts, and the majority of all courts, give particular weight to the financial relationship between the hired and hiring parties.[4] For example, the failure of a horse-related business to "extend employment benefits or to pay any payroll taxes to one of its workers is 'highly indicative' that the individual is an independent contractor."[5] Similarly, a stable owner's "tax and benefit treatment" of its workers can be virtual admissions of the status of its workers. If the stable is paying a stable-hand regularly, he or she will most likely be considered an employee, while the "absence of regular, periodic payments is an indicia of independent contractor status."[6]

Fair Labor Standards Act

While most federal statutes utilize the common-law agency doctrine, not all do, including the two which are arguably the most relevant to horse-related businesses: the Fair Labor Standards Act of 1938 ("FLSA"), and the Internal Revenue Code ("IRC").

1. Fair Labor Standards Act

The FLSA, sometimes referred to as the Wage and Hour Law, establishes minimum wage, overtime pay, recordkeeping, and youth employment standards for employees of most equine facilities, but it does not apply to their independent contractors. FLSA cases are decided utilizing a broader definition of employee than the common law.[7] In FLSA cases, courts consider the "economic realities" of the relationship between the worker and the alleged employer.[8] The focal point is whether the worker "is economically dependent on the business to which he renders service or is, as a matter of economic reality, in business for himself."[9]

The emphasis on "economic reality" has led courts to develop a six-factor test to determine whether a worker is an employee or an independent contractor. These factors are called the "Silk factors" in reference to the U.S. Supreme Court case from which they are originally derived, United States v. Silk, 331 U.S. 704 (1947). These factors are:

(1) The degree of control that the putative employer has over the manner in which the work is performed;

(2) The worker's opportunities for profit or loss dependent on his managerial skill;

(3) The worker's investment in equipment or material, or his employment of other workers;

(4) The degree of skill required for the work;

(5) The permanence of the working relationship; and

(6) The degree to which the services rendered are an integral part of the putative employer's business.[10]

As with the common law test shown above, no single one of these factors is dispositive.[11] It requires a common-sense approach that recognizes "that we are dealing with human beings and with a statute that is intended to secure to them the fruits of their toil and exertion."[12] In other words, the definition of employee under the FLSA will be applied broadly to make sure those working for others are covered by the statutes mandates.

2. Internal Revenue Code

The Internal Revenue Code defines "employee" to include "any individual who, under the usual common law rules applicable in determining the employer-employee relationship, has the status of an employee."[13] IRS regulations provide detailed guidance for determining whether a person providing services to an individual is an employee of that individual rather than an independent contractor.[14]

Section 31.3401(c)-1(b), Employment Tax Regs., defines the employer/employee relationship as follows:

(b) Generally the relationship of employer and employee exists when the person for whom services are performed has the right to control and direct the individual who performs the services, not only as to the result to be accomplished by the work but also as to the details and means by which that result is accomplished. That is, an employee is subject to the will and control of the employer not only as to what shall be done but how it shall be done. In this connection, it is not necessary that the employer actually direct or control the manner in which the services are performed; it is sufficient if he [or she] has the right to do so. The right to discharge is also an important factor indicating that the person possessing that right is an employer. Other factors characteristic of an employer, but not necessarily present in every case, are the furnishing of tools and the furnishing of a place to work to the individual who performs the services. In general, if an individual is subject to the control or direction of another merely as to the result to be accomplished by the work and not as to the means and methods for accomplishing the result, he [or she] is not an employee.

The Court of Appeals for the Fourth Circuit, federal appellate court for Maryland, has also identified the following seven factors in determining whether an employment relationship exists in a tax context:

(1) The degree of control exercised by the principal over the details of the work;

(2) which party invests in the facilities used in the work;

(3) the opportunity of the individual for profit or loss;

(4) whether or not the principal has the right to discharge the individual;

(5) whether the work is part of the principal's regular business;

(6) the permanency of the relationship; and

(7) the relationship the parties believe they are creating.[15]

Again, no one of these factors is controlling. In the case of the IRC, particular weight is given to the control the stable exerts over its workers.[16] While this nuisance may be subtle and, more often than not, will not be outcome determinative, horse-related business owners should be aware of it.

Maryland Law

As with federal law, Maryland law often distinguishes between whether an equine facility worker is an employee or independent contractor. To make this determination, Maryland courts will often look to case law interpreting analogous federal statutes and adopt their holdings. Thus, the analysis used in determining whether a worker is an employee is not fundamentally different under federal and state law, unless otherwise specified by statute.

Another important issue that arises with respect to those engaged by horse-related businesses in Maryland is that of vicarious liability. Although the issue is not one of employer-employee but, rather, that of master-servant, the concept is similar. A principal is vicariously liable for the negligence of its agent when the two share a master-servant relationship, but not when the agent is merely an independent contractor of the principal.[17]

This is also known as the doctrine of *respondeat superior.* Under this doctrine, the master or employer may be held liable for the torts of a servant or employee, but only if the employee was acting within the scope of employment when the tortious activity occurred.[18] Whether the relation of the parties is that of master and servant, or employer and independent contractor, depends upon the facts of such particular case, and is to be determined by the application of the appropriate principles of law.[19] Those principles are fairly well settled and are as follows:

1. the selection and engagement of the servant;

2. the payment of wages;

3. the power of dismissal;

4. the power of control of the servant's conduct; and

5. whether the work is a part of the regular business of the employer.[20]

The decisive factor, however, is whether the employer has the right to control and direct the servant in the performance of his work and the manner in which it is done. For a master "controls or has the right to control the physical conduct of the [servant] in the performance of the service."[21]

But the existence of a master-servant relationship is not enough. For an equine facility to be liable for its servant's tort, the negligent act itself must have occurred within the scope of the tortfeasor's employment. Although "there are few, if any, absolutes" involved in determining whether an employee's acts occurred within the "scope of employment," the general test in Maryland is that the acts must have been authorized and in furtherance of the employer's business.[22] "Authorized" in this context does not mean actually sanctioned, but rather that the act was "incident to the performance of the duties entrusted to [the employee] by the master, even though in opposition to his express and positive orders."[23]

Various factors come into play when making this inquiry, including: (1) whether the conduct is the kind the servant is employed to perform; (2) whether it occurred during a period not unreasonably disconnected from the authorized period of employment; (3) whether it occurred in the vicinity of the authorized area of employment; and (4) whether it was actuated, at least in part, by a purpose to serve the employer.[24] In the case of intentional torts, the employee will be found to have been acting beyond the scope of employment where the acts were personal and departed from the purpose of promoting the employer's interests.[25] This is particularly true where the employee's conduct was "unprovoked, highly unusual, and quite outrageous."[26]

CHAPTER 12

Resolving Disputes

*"There are myriad methods for settling disputes –
discuss with your attorney the options and explore
which option is best for you!"*

Inevitably, even with the best of intentions, and even with the most well written agreements (or oral understandings), a dispute will arise, an accident will occur, and damages will be sustained. The need to resolve the dispute, in all honesty, actually goes beyond the compensation of losses. In the "world of horses," there is a strong need to preserve the relationship between the parties, whether it's a familial one, or strictly a working business relationship. It is rather predictable that the parties' paths will cross again, whether at the next sporting event, horse show, horse sale, in the barn, or during personal pursuits. And, if nothing else, the nature of the conflict and the manner in which it was resolved (satisfactorily or not) will be made known to other equestrians and "interested parties" involved in that particular realm of horse activities.

Resolving conflicts in the equine industry is no different than resolving a dispute in any other walk of life. The significant difference here is the nature of the relationship between the disputing parties, their past relationship, the current circumstances, and the future interaction of the individuals are significant concerns to be considered.

For the majority of disagreements, disputes are handled in the most simplest of manners: face to face. Usually, the conflict is resolved much in the same way as how the agreement underlying the dispute may have been formed whether informally with a handshake on each other's "word" or formally through a written contract.

But often times the personal resolution of a disagreement cannot be reached and suddenly cries of "It's not the money, it's the principle of the matter!" or "That so-and-so needs to be taught a lesson, I don't care how much it costs me!" are heard. But the bottom-line is, in reality it IS about the money. And more often than not, the average horse-person does not have the expendable income to teach another the lesson he or she so sorely wants taught. But nevertheless, damages have been sustained and someone needs to be held responsible. Enter the legal community.

How Best to Resolve Differences

The variety of resolving differences really is only limited by one's resources and one's imagination. In this litigious society of ours, the disputing parties almost always feel the best and only way to obtain satisfaction is through the court system. Hopefully, the need to run into court will not be the first thought when it comes to resolving a conflict. Still, sometimes the only way of resolving some disputes is through the judicial system.

Attorneys, mediators, arbitrators, and the court system certainly are the "arsenal" for resolving disputes. However, with the limited resource of money and time, the individuals wishing to resolve a wrong would be wise to consider alternatives before resorting to litigation. In Maryland, alternative dispute resolution is defined as "the process of resolving matters in pending litigation through a settlement conference, neutral case evaluation, neutral fact-finding, arbitration, mediation, other non-judicial dispute resolution, or combination of those processes."[1]

Attorneys are trained to assist their clients in determining the legal ramifications of unfortunate circumstances. However, not all attorneys are trained in effectively using the variety of methods of resolving disputes. Choosing an attorney who can best suit the needs of the individual should be taken with deliberate thought and careful consideration. Having an attorney that understands not only the underlying issues of the dispute, but who also understands the subject of horses and the equine industry can expedite the resolution between the parties.

Initially, an attorney will counsel the aggrieved party (traditionally referred to as "plaintiff" or "defendant") on the legal consequences of the issue and assist in a cost-benefit analysis on resolving the dispute. This provides the individual with information to determine whether or not the issue should be pursued further. However, no attorney can guarantee any particular outcome for any particular dispute; other influences have an affect on the outcome which is not in the control of the attorney.

In Maryland, attorneys must advise their client on the available methods for resolving a dispute so that the client is educated and informed prior to making a decision as to which method is best for their particular situation.[2] Remember, it is not the responsibility of the attorney to determine which method is best for you! That decision does, and should, rest with the client. At the end of the day, it is the parties involved in the dispute that will be living with the consequences of the resolution, not the attorneys. Carefully evaluating what is involved (time, money, ongoing relationship between the parties) and what is at stake in order to come to a resolution should be considered prior to filing that complaint in court.

Settling the Disagreement

Depending on who you talk to, statistically, 80% or more of cases filed for litigation will settle prior to coming before a judge or jury. Meanwhile, the time and expenses expended on these cases will vary depending on how quickly the two parties can come to an agreement to settle their differences.

Aside from using "self-help" methods (as in directly communicating with the other party or acting as a pro se [3] litigant in court) the aide of an attorney can be very beneficial to the aggrieved parties. Not only will the attorney help with identifying the methods available for resolution, but will apply their training and expertise in assisting those seeking resolution. The attorney should take into consideration not only the basic legal principles involved, but scrutinize the motivation of the individual seeking recourse. Which methods should be considered to obtain the best outcome for the individual seeking assistance will be determined not only by the factual circumstances of the conflict, but also the degree of involvement by the client, the financial ability to pursue recourse, the motivation for resolution, the client's ability (or inability) to work cooperatively throughout the process, as well as the other party's degree of involvement, motivation, resources, and temperament.

However, before marching down to the courthouse of this State (or any other), consider other possibilities of resolving the dispute. Depending on the individual's need for control of the process (or the desire to have others control the process) as well as what outcome is truly sought, the method of resolving the dispute is only limited by the aggrieved party's financial resources and motivation.

Methods of Dispute Resolution

The methods of dispute resolution vary in degree of client involvement, professional assistance, as well as the manner of communication in the process of resolving a conflict. The following methods are described below from the most primary (direct) to the most complex (litigation). Generally, the courts will not require parties to participate in alternative dispute resolutions once they have filed suit, unless, of course, the parties have agreed previously (contractually or otherwise) to first resolve their dispute using some method other than litigation prior to filing suit. However, the courts are very encouraging to having disputing parties resolve their differences prior to or even without coming before the bench. And in some circumstances, alternative dispute methods may be court-ordered.

(1) Direct

This process is the simplest of all conflict resolution. It is primarily a face-to-face, sit-down discussion between the aggrieved parties in which they engage in negotiating their differences. The parties may engage the services of an attorney perhaps only to draft the agreement reached between the parties, review the legal aspects of the terms and conditions, and to advise the client of the legal rights and responsibilities of each party of that particular agreement. If a breach of this agreement occurs, contract law would prevail.

Direct resolution works best if the matter is not complex, does not involve a lot of money damages, the two parties can calmly and reasonably communicate with one another, and they both have the desire to preserve ongoing business and/or personal relationships with one another.

(2) Mediation

Mediation is a beneficial method of resolving disputes when the parties involved have difficulty communicating directly with one another, could use the assistance of a communication facilitator, and the primary issue of money damages may not be the only underlying conflict. The value of a neutral individual trained in assisting those in conflict to come to a resolution based on their own terms and conditions can be found through the mediation process.

The mediation process is an informal, voluntary procedure in which all discussions and communications are confidential. The parties involved in the dispute are ultimately the decision-makers on what is contained in the final agreement. On occasion, parties may bring with them an attorney as legal support. It should be the parties who are in disagreement holding the discussion and making the decisions, not the attorneys. However, there are times that a judge will order mediation for cases docketed in their court, which are often scheduled prior to a settlement conference. These sessions are still an informal (without court intervention) process of resolving disputes and are still considered voluntary in the sense that any of the parties may chose not to appear for the mediation session.

Mediation sessions generally run a minimum of two hours. More than one session may be necessary, depending on the complexity of the issue(s) involved. A mediator, particularly one already familiar with the terminology of equines and the industry, may be best suited for those involved in disputes involving horses. However, any well-trained mediator can assist the parties through the process of mediation.

Whether or not a mediation agreement is considered enforceable may depend largely on how "mediation" is defined. Black's Law Dictionary defines mediation as "(A) method of non-binding dispute resolution involving a neutral third party who tries to help the disputing parties reach a mutually agreeable solution."[4] Maryland courts have stated "(M)ediation is a conciliative process in which a mediator assists the parties in reaching their own solution or agreement."[5] Maryland Rules of Procedure defines mediation as a "means in which the parties work with one or more impartial mediators who, without providing legal advice, assists the parties in reaching their own agreement for the resolution of the dispute or issues in the dispute…"[6]

The issue of enforceability arises when the parties consider a mediation agreement binding and then one of the parties choses to breach that agreement. Using contract law to enforce a mediation agreement will take the parties out of the "neutral realm" of the resolving their dispute and into the courtroom for resolving the breach.

An agreement resulting from mediation would be considered a contract. "An express contract has been defined as an 'an actual agreement of the parties, the terms of which are openly uttered or declared at the time of making it, being stated in distinct and explicit language, either orally or in writing.' An implied contract is an agreement which legitimately can be inferred from intention of the parties as evidenced by the circumstances and 'the ordinary course of dealing and the common understanding of men.'"[7]

The enforceability of mediation agreements will vary among jurisdictions. Other states have developed case law regarding the enforceability of a mediation agreement. (See "Appendix Three," page 195, for a summary of cases as it pertains to the enforceability of mediation agreements.) Maryland courts have not yet ruled as to the enforceability of mediation agreements, although the courts do recognize the validity and value of mediation clauses within courts. Judges even encourage litigants to consider mediation prior to bringing the case before the court for final decision. It appears, at this time, that the law of contract will dictate whether or not a mediation agreement is enforceable. And it goes without saying that putting the parties' understanding in writing is the best method of preserving the enforceability of such agreements.

(3) Settlement Conference

The settlement conference is often scheduled by the Clerk of the court on the calendar events of a pending case. Maryland defines the settlement conference process as "a conference at which the parties, their attorneys, or both appear before an impartial person to discuss the issues and position of the parties in the action in an attempt to resolve the dispute or issues in the dispute by agreement or by means other than trial. A settlement conference may include neutral case evaluation and neutral fact-finding, and the impartial person may recommend the terms of an agreement."[8] The impartial person often times is an active judge of the court, but not the judge whom would hear the case in court.

(4) Arbitration

Arbitration has been integrated into many commercial contracts which most people are familiar (i.e. real estate purchase agreements). Arbitration is more formal and elaborate than mediation, as it often involves the complexity of discovery and evidence, it's very much based on preparing for a court trial. The arbitrator may be a retired judge, lawyer, or another professional trained in the process of arbitration.

Maryland defines arbitration as "a process in which (1) the parties appear before one or more impartial arbitrators and present evidence and argument supporting their respective positions, and (2) the arbitrators render a decision in the form of an award that is not binding, unless the parties agree otherwise in writing."[9]

Binding arbitration finalizes the decision between the parties and is not appealable to the court system. Non-binding arbitration permits the parties to appeal the decision to the courts for further deliberation and fact-finding. Arbitration may take months to complete from the time of the initial scheduling to the conclusion of the decision-making process, as the attorneys will be preparing the presentation of their client's argument to the arbitrator much as they would to a judge or jury.

(5) Collaboration

The collaborative process is a "structured, voluntary, non-adversarial dispute resolution process in which the parties and their lawyers sign an agreement to negotiate in good faith giving consideration to the interests of all parties, to resolve their dispute without resorting to a court imposed resolution, to disclose all relevant information, and to engage neutral experts, as needed, for assistance in resolving issues. The process envisions the use of other non-adversarial dispute resolution methods such as mediation to facilitate negotiations when needed. The written agreement must provide that the lawyers shall withdraw if the collaborative process is terminated."[10]

Not all disputes are suitable for the collaborative process. A trained collaborative attorney will assess the client's objectives and determine whether there is any inconsistency with the principles of collaboration which would undermine the process. The collaborative attorney represents the client in a zealous manner as their advocate and protector of legal rights, but works in tandem with the other party's attorney, in a team setting which may involve other collaboratively trained professionals, such as a business appraiser, financial specialist, or communication specialist.

In Maryland, the collaborative process has been embraced by many of the courts in the realm of domestic relations law. The civil law application continues to develop as more attorneys are trained in this specialized method of dispute resolution. (See "Appendix Four," page 201, for a resource list of collaborative trained attorneys.)

(6) Litigation

An aggrieved party can approach the litigation process in one of two ways, as either a pro se litigant or with the aide of an attorney. The court fees involved will vary depending on the jurisdiction. The attorney fees will also vary - sometimes an attorney may offer his or her services on a sliding fee scale or even on a *pro bono*[11] basis. Regardless, the expense of time spent following the rules and protocols of the judicial system will be consuming.

When alternative dispute resolution methods have failed, or were never suitable to the case originally, the aggrieved individual has the difficult choice of either walking away from the conflict or addressing the issues through a finder of fact (judge or jury). The complexities of the litigation procedure are often confusing and frustrating to the average citizen. This is when a well-trained attorney can benefit the individual wishing to resolve a dispute. However, even in the best of circumstances (strong facts, facts supported by law, and solid evidence), a civil dispute may be less than satisfactory when the conflict involves individuals who will continue to be involved in the same tight-circle of associates, friends, and businesses.

In Review

Horses are high risk. Period. Whether used for pleasure or as a business asset. And the expenses of maintaining the animals can be extraordinary at times. Relationships among and between those involved in the horse industry runs far and deep.

There are a myriad of methods for resolving conflict. And when it comes to the horse industry, preserving a mutually-agreeable relationship can be tantamount. Either as a horse enthusiast or business-person, carefully consider the long-term interests you have when a conflict arises. Consider the numerous methods of resolving the dispute before rushing to your attorney to file suit. As an attorney, a thoughtful evaluation of your client's needs will help you guide your client in selecting the best method of dispute resolution. A "good-enough" outcome that can satisfy both parties will be beneficial to all involved in the long run.

CHAPTER 13

Business Organizations

*"Consult with an attorney to be certain your equine
activity is a bona fide business and not a hobby
disguised as a business."*

Business or hobby? For many, this question may seem irrelevant. However, if you are considering operating a business (or currently are operating one) you must be able to demonstrate to the IRS that the activity is "engaged in for profit." If your business continues to lose money every year for a number of years, you must be prepared to prove to the IRS that the operation will be profitable in the future. Pre-planning and the use of "best business practices" will assist you in the on-going operations of your business. Utilizing outside professional advice (legal, financial, and industrial) demonstrates to the IRS that your operation is organized for business, and not hobby, purposes. This is especially vital for those engaging in equine activities and businesses.

The type of equine activity, the selection of business entity, tax status classification, and practices will all be considered by the Internal Revenue Service (IRS) in the event your tax return is selected for an audit. There is no one criterion that confers more credence than another to a claim of business operation. The IRS will examine all aspects of the particular "business operation" in determining whether or not it meets the standards of a business or a hobby.

Throughout this book we have discussed, among myriad topics, the importance of contracts and compliance with regulations, employment law, insurance, and licensing. The IRS has established guidelines to assist an individual embarking on a business enterprise. Whether for profit or non-profit, the IRS looks at specific factors to determine if an activity exists for business purposes. Equine activities are scrutinized by the IRS, as often happens, a hobby may develop into a business, or be disguised as a business in an effort to obtain favorable tax deductions.[1]

When Congress enacted the 1969 Tax Reform Act various classifications of organizations developed. Along with these distinctions in organizational models, the Act modified the law on "activities engaged in for profit" and the IRS subsequently issued regulations for assessing when an activity is a business or a hobby (an activity engaged in not-for-profit). As detailed in the IRS Publication 535, the IRS is very specific on its guidelines in determining a business or hobby activity and the impact for non-compliance can be severe to a small equine business owner. It is a difficult business in which to turn a profit. Equine service providers more often see red ink than black on their end-of-year balance sheets. The expense of operating an equine business is tied up in the inventory of livestock and the maintenance and care of the livestock (including such auxiliary services as a veterinarian, trainer, and farrier, as well as tack and feed), leaving very little for the bottom line.[2]

Best Business Practices

Approaching your equine activity as a business requires forethought and action. Building a "business team" to assist you in your undertaking is a first step the IRS (or other government authority) will view as characteristic of a serious business. Consider these professionals as part of your personalized business team: an attorney, a banker, a CPA (or accounting firm), an insurance agent/broker, and industry specific agencies such as the Maryland Horse Industry Board or the Maryland Extension Cooperative Services, for example.

Hiring professionals that are both experts in their field, and are familiar with equine activities and operations, will enhance your credibility with the IRS. This demonstrates one of the crucial factors the IRS looks for when determining whether or not an equine activity is seriously a business operation or a hobby. It's also critical to your day-to-day operations to have a professional you can contact with questions or concerns. Building a professional relationship on a personal level may just be the key to obtaining a crucial loan or quick response you may not otherwise get from a "faceless," no-first-name institutional service provider.

A primary concern any horse business owner should consider is the IRS "hobby loss rule." Internal Revenue Code Section 183 ("Activities Not Engaged in for Profit) limits deductions that can be claimed when an activity is not engaged in for profit.[3] IRC 183 is sometimes referred to as the "hobby loss rule."[4] See Chapter 10 for a detailing of the nine factors. The IRS will presume an activity is carried on for-profit if the business shows a profit during at least three of the last five tax years (including the current year), or in the case of equine activities consisting primarily of breeding, showing, training, or racing horses, if the business shows a profit for at least two of the last seven years.[5]

At the 2008 annual Equine Law Conference, two very wise and experienced attorneys presented on the subject of distinguishing an equine activity as a bona fide horse business."[6] Messrs. Richard Craigo and Paul Husband acquainted the participants with the formalities of an IRS audit, detailed the nuances of the IRS guidelines and recommended how best to approach a horse business with the intent of addressing any potential IRS challenges. Of course, many businesses begin operation before the business owner or manager has consulted with an attorney to assess and review the various aspects of funning a business. However, it is never too late to analyze your operations and ensure your practices comply with the IRS guidelines. Along with their summary of the IRC 183, they provided some very practical advice. Much of what they presented was basic business practices with a whole lot of horse sense!

Financial accountability is extremely important in managing a business. Always keep a separate checking account for your business from your personal or other business accounts. Personal and business funds should not be commingled. However, as long as an accurate accounting of the separate expenses can be shown, not having a separate business account should not necessarily indicate your business is your hobby.

In the event of an audit, the IRS will ask for certain documentation that reinforces the notion that this is a bona fide business operation. A business plan that was developed from the onset of the operation, along with periodic reviews and updates, demonstrates the forethought and the intent of making a profit from your activity. Obviously, a business plan kept in one's mind is not easily accessed by the IRS and the lack of a written plan may just scream "hobby!" The business plan should include your goals, a mission statement, targeted market, analysis of similar operations in your region, key success factors, milestones, a vision of the business, financial statement and annual budget, and an evaluation of your risks and what your profit potential may be.

Keeping accurate books and records is a given for any business activity. But often times the bookkeeping is pushed aside when the task at hand of managing an equine business dominates the clock. If possible, consider hiring a professional accountant or bookkeeping services to maintain your records. Explore the possibility of business management software; there's even equine management software available to assist in a "horse-by-horse" accounting. And by all means, retain all prior tax returns. Any record that can demonstrate your intent to turn a profit will be helpful in the occasion of an audit.

Consulting with experts and self-education also indicates the intent to operate a successful (i.e., profitable) business. In the horse industry, you can avail yourself of the guidance and expertise of extension services personnel, Department of Agriculture professionals, equine association and industry leaders, and an equine-savvy attorney! Self-education through seminars, industry organization membership (such as the Maryland Horse Council), and subscription to industry-specific periodicals is an indicator of an intent to turn a profit.

Along with self-education is keeping a time log of your participation in the business operations. This can include keeping track of the time spent on self-education (reading articles, attending meetings, etc.) and managing the affairs of the business (supervising hired help, etc.). This may appear a bit overwhelming or even a waste of time to an individual with little extra time to call their own. But the ability to demonstrate to the IRS that this is indeed a for-profit activity that requires your full attention will prove golden in the event an audit of your activities arises.

Operate the activity as a business through a business entity rather than as a sole proprietor. Business entities such as limited liability companies or "S" corporations lend credibility that the horses are there for a profit, and not just a hobby with a business name.

Anyone involved with horses as a business can attest to the number of unforeseen hardships that occur. Memorialize these hardships (such as a barn roof that collapsed in a snowstorm or the loss of boarders or students due to an economic downturn). In the event of consecutive loss years, this documentation will assist the IRS in determining the reasons for a lack of profit. Don't rely on your memory to keep these events fresh for recall. Put it down on paper!

The value of a horse is typically whatever price one is willing to pay. But appraisals can assist in creating a record of a horse's appreciation in value (as it continues its training and career) even if the business shows a loss. Better to spend a little money obtaining that professional appraisal to record the horse's (increased or decreased) value than trying to explain to the IRS later why you continued to throw good money after bad.

Minimizing the appearance of pleasure or recreation may be a more difficult factor to overcome. Most people involved with horse businesses are involved because they like the animal or the particular sport or activity the horse generates. Horse racing activities rarely involves the owner riding (or driving) the horse, although it's not unheard of with Standardbreds, so this particular business essentially eliminates the pleasure factor by default. For farm owners with swimming pools and tennis courts on the property, it may be a bit more challenging convincing the IRS agent that the farm is a working operation and not just another aspect of personal recreation. Even tougher are those business operations which engage the services of the owner or family members to show the horses. Although the IRS may more closely examine the business activities, if the business purpose of the individual's participation is clearly stated (here is where the business plan can help) the extra scrutiny can be overcome.

A last piece of advice from the experiences of my learned colleagues, Messers. Craigo and Husband, was the matter of "grouping" activities when filing tax returns. A top-notch CPA or tax attorney may be able to assist you in determining whether particular "sub-activities" or functions of your equine business aid in your tax liabilities if grouped with the primary business. "Treasury Regulation § 1.469(c)(1) provides that multiple trades or business may be treated as a single activity if they constitute an 'appropriate economic unit' based on 'all facts and circumstances.'"[7] The five factors the IRS evaluates in determining if a grouping of activities constitutes an "appropriate economic unit" include:

- Similarities or differences in the types of business (e.g., if selling tack or horse gifts goes along with a boarding facility);

- Extent of common control (e.g. is the gift shop operations overseen by the primary business owner);

- Extent of common ownership (e.g. is the tack shop operated by a different individual who is not an owner or member of the primary equine activity);

- Geographic location (e.g. where are the various divisions or functions located in relation to the primary business); and

- Interdependence of the activities (e.g. whether or not the functions are closely related in function and purpose).

Choice of Business Entity

When deciding on the type of operational entity for your business, you should carefully consider these factors: (1) the nature of your business, (2) the individual(s) involved in the management of your business, (3) how capital will be raised and invested into the company, (4) continuity and transferability, (5) the risks and liabilities of your particular business, and (6) taxation issues (state and federal). Other considerations include staffing (the use of employees, independent contractors, volunteers, etc.), the types of licenses required for your particular business operation, insurance considerations, and the development and ongoing use of sound business practices, including the use of "outside" professionals and resources.

A sole proprietorship and general partnership are business organizations that do not require legal entity formation. The State of Maryland only requires these forms of businesses to comply with any State and local licensing, regulations, and taxation requirements as may be pertinent to the particular business purpose. The legal business entities which require registration with the Department of Assessments and Taxation (SDAT) are corporations, limited liability companies, limited partnerships and limited liability partnerships. If a legal business entity has been formed in a state other than Maryland, but now operates here, that business is required to register as a "foreign entity" and submit the requisite fees for the privilege of doing business in Maryland.

The most common equine business operations are corporations, limited liability companies, and limited liability partnerships, and in some cases, non-profit corporations. The "family farm" designation is increasingly popular for those who qualify. A summary of the general aspects of the various business operations and some of the pros and cons to consider when selecting an appropriate business entity follows.

Sole Proprietorship

Typical of many horse business operations, a sole proprietorship is an unincorporated business that is owned by one individual. It is the simplest form of business organization. The business has no existence apart from the owner. It is not its own entity. The liabilities of the business are the proprietor's liabilities. The owner undertakes the risks of the business for all assets owned, whether used in the business or personally owned. Income and expenses of the business are included on the individual's tax return.

No documentation for this type of business operation is required to be filed with the Maryland State Department of Assessments and Taxation ("SDAT"). No annual report fee is required, but the filing of an annual personal property tax return is still required. An Employer Identification Number (EIN) assigned by the IRS is not available as the sole proprietor is taxed under his/her own social security number.

Pros

- Inexpensive to start up.

- Simple to run.

- No double taxation on profits.

- Not required to file MD annual report fee; but must file personal property tax return.

Cons

- Owner has unlimited personal liability for business liabilities.

- Business has unlimited liability for personal liabilities.

- Ownership is limited to one person and dissolved upon death of proprietor.

Partnership (General)

General partnerships are also unincorporated businesses. A partnership is the business relationship that develops when two or more persons agree to join together to carry on a trade or business. Each person contributes money, property, labor, or skill, and expects to share in the profits and losses of the business. A partnership does not have to be formalized in writing with the State of Maryland. However, a Partnership Agreement is highly recommended for use as the company's internal operational document.

A partnership must file an annual information return to report the income, deductions, gains, losses etc., from its operations, but it does not pay income tax. Instead, it "passes through" any profits or losses to its partners. Each partner includes his or her share of the partnership's income or loss on his or her individual tax return.

Partners are not employees and are not issued a Form W-2. EINs are not issued to general partnership as the partners are assessed taxes through their individual tax returns. The partnership entity must furnish copies of I.R.S. Schedule K-1 (Form 1065) to the partners by the date Form 1065 is required to be filed, including extensions. No State annual report fee is required; however, partnerships are still required to file a personal property tax return annually.

Joint Venture Or Syndication

A joint venture or syndication is a partnership. This is a popular format for individuals who may be interested in the temporary management of a race horse, stallion, or brood mare. This partnership is typically between two or more individuals and/or business entities, (partnerships, corporations, LLCs, or LLPs). The purpose of a joint venture or syndication relationship generally is to share the risks or expertise on a specific project or group of projects. Like a general partnership, this relationship is not incorporated. State and federal filing requirements as applicable to a partnership are applicable to a joint venture. It is highly recommended that joint ventures operate through a Partnership Agreement. Syndication requires similar contractual documents to detail the rights, responsibilities, financial obligations, and other requirements for those involved.

Limited Partnership (LP) And
Limited Liability Partnership (LLP)

Although general partnerships are recognized as "informal" (unincorporated) business entities, the State of Maryland recognizes the more formalized partnership arrangements known as a Limited Partnership (LP) and a Limited Liability Partnership (LLP).

A Limited Partnership (LP) requires one partner to serve as the general partner (serves as the managing partner) and the other partner to serve as a limited (or "silent") partner. There is no limit to the number of partners in an LP. However, at least one partner must be the general partner and one partner the limited partner. The limited partner, although sharing in the profits and losses as any partnership, is prohibited from serving as an active manager of the business. In "exchange" for foregoing any managerial relationship, the government grants the limited partner full liability protection against his/her personal assets. Limited Partnerships are required to register with SDAT through the filing of a "Certificate of Limited Partnership." SDAT also requires annual report fees and personal property returns.

Limited Liability Partnerships are required to have a Resident Agent on file. Filing fees are required. Annual report fee is required. Personal Property return is also required. Partnership Agreements are highly recommended as the company's internal operational document.

Pros

- Very flexible form of business.

- Permits ownership by more than one individual.

- Avoids double taxation.

- Few legal formalities for its maintenance.

- General Partnership not required to pay MD annual report fee; personal property tax return required.

- Partners have unlimited personal liability for business losses.

Cons

- Partnership is legally responsible for the business acts of each partner.

- General partnership interest may not be sold or transferred without consent of all partners.

- Partnership dissolves upon death of a general partner.

- LP and LLP are required to pay MD annual report fee; annual personal property tax return also required.

Corporation

In forming a corporation, prospective owners (shareholders or stockholders) exchange money, property, or both, for the corporation's capital stock. A corporation generally takes the same deductions as a sole proprietorship to figure its taxable income. A corporation can also take special deductions.

Corporations are subject to double-taxation. The profit of a corporation is taxed to the corporation when earned and then taxed to the shareholders when distributed as dividends. Although stockholders have limited liability for the debts and actions of corporations, stockholders cannot deduct any loss of the corporation.

In Maryland, stock, non-stock, and close corporations are required to file Articles of Incorporation (as do Religious corporations, and Tax-exempt Non-Stock corporations) with SDAT. Filing fees and a resident agent are required. Annual report fees also are required. Personal property return required. Religious and Tax-exempt Non-Stock corporations are not required to file annul reports, but must file personal property returns. All corporation types are required to operate through Bylaws. A Corporation is required by the IRS to obtain an EIN.

Close Corporation

Many long-establish equine business operations originated as a close corporation. Generally, the close corporation has a limited number of stockholders who actively participate in the business, typically have close personal relationships (often time family members) among the stockholders, and does not have an established market for the corporation's stock (will not be "going public"). Close corporation is one in which the stock is subject to certain transfer restrictions, and the election to operate as a close corporation must be established by the unanimous vote of stockholders.

This entity must specifically state it is a "close" corporation when filing its Articles of Incorporation. A close corporation is taxed in the same manner as a general corporation. It also has the same SDAT and IRS filing requirements.

S Corporation

An eligible domestic ("in-state") corporation can avoid double taxation (once to the shareholders and again to the corporation) by electing to be treated as an "S Corporation." Generally an S corporation is exempt from federal income tax other than tax on certain capital gains and passive income. On their tax returns, the S corporation's shareholders include their share of the corporation's separately stated items of income, deduction, loss, and credit, and their share of non-separately stated income or loss. Your accountant/CPA can explain these details to you.

An S Corp must comply with all SDAT and IRS filing requirements.

Pros
- Provides limited liability to owners (stockholders/ shareholders).
- Easy to transfer ownership (close corp. has limitations).
- Easy to add additional owners/investors (close corp. has limitations).

Cons
- Is more costly to set up and maintain.
- Requires formal dissolution.
- Requires separate tax returns.
- Subject to double taxation (Subchapter S Corporation are exempt).
- Required to pay MD annual report fee.

Limited Liability Company (LLC)

A LLC is a very popular business entity for smaller equine business operations. "Owners" or participants of an LLC are actually called "Members." Members may include individuals, corporations, other LLCs and even foreign ("out of state") entities. There is no maximum number of members. Maryland recognizes the "single member" LLC; having only one participant/member.

Limited Liability Companies provides its members the corporate-like protection of personal assets from the entity's liability for debts and actions of the LLC, yet it allows the LLC to choose a more favorable taxation status than that of a corporation. No member is personally liable for the obligations of the LLC, whether arising in contract or tort. And there is no double taxation.

Other appealing features of the LLC are those which are more similar in nature to a partnership arrangement; providing management flexibility and the benefit of pass-through taxation. An LLC has the option to be taxed as a "sole proprietorship," "partnership," or "corporation." If a single member LLC is formed, the tax option will be sole proprietorship. If two or more members form an LLC, the tax options are partnership or corporation.

Sole proprietorships and general or limited partnerships are easily converted to an LLC. It is simply a matter of organizing as a limited liability company (single or multi-member). However, corporations are not convertible. The corporation entity must first be dissolved before an LLC or other business entity is formed in its place.

Maryland requires Articles of Organization to be filed with SDAT. An LLC obtains its own EIN. A resident agent is required, as are filing fees and annual fees. LLCs enter into Operating Agreements ("OA"); similar to a corporation's bylaws. The OA is the company's internal operational document. The LLC must also file a personal property return with the State of Maryland annually.

Pros
• Very flexible form of business.

- Permits ownership by one individual or more.

- Avoids double taxation.

- May choose type of taxation (including sole proprietor, partnership, or "S" corporation).

- Few legal formalities for its maintenance.

- Provides limited liability to members.

- Flexibility of ownership transfers.

- Easy to add additional members.

Cons
- Formal dissolution required.

- Required to pay MD annual report fee.

Family Farm

A family farm may file as a Corporation, Limited Liability Company, or a Partnership. See above "pros and cons" for determining the best entity for your family farm. Pursuant to the Maryland Code, a farm may qualify as a "family farm" under the following five conditions:

(1)   Is a domestic entity [i.e. files the appropriate charter document]; AND

(2)(i)   1. The property [currently or within one year of filing entity] that is owned qualifies for agricultural use assessment under MD Tax-Property Article § 8-209 *; AND

2. Owns only agriculturally or residentially assessed real property and personal property that is used for agricultural purposes; or

(ii) Owns only personal property that is used for agricultural or agricultural marketing purposes; AND

(3)   Is controlled, managed, and operated by:

(i) One individual who has an equity interest in the entity; or

(ii) Two or more individuals who have an equity interest in the entity and who share its assets and earnings; AND

(4) Is declared in a charter provision to be a family farm; AND

(5) Has no assets other than those described in item (2).

* The Dept. of Agriculture defines such property as land that is actively used (actually and primarily used) for farm or agricultural purposes, is zoned for agricultural use, and gross income is derived from agricultural use.

Other Maryland Recognized Business Entities:

- Non-stock Corporations (i.e., non-profit) – many horse rescue operations choose this format
- Religious Corporations
- Private Foundations
- Agricultural Cooperatives
- Electric and Transportation Cooperatives
- Consumer Cooperatives
- Cooperative Housing Corporations
- Real Estate Investment Trusts (REIT)
- Business Trusts
- Foreign Corps, Foreign LPs, Foreign LLPs, Foreign LLCs
- Professional Corporations (chtd, P.A., P.C.) Includes: architect, attorney, certified public account, chiropractor, dentist, osteopath, physician, podiatrist, professional engineer, psychologist, licensed real estate broker/ salesperson, or veterinarian.

The above business entities have similar requirements as the basic business entities described more fully, but also have additional requirements particular to its organizational structure.

If you are contemplating starting an equine business, there are several issues to consider as you undertake this endeavor -- as noted throughout this book. If you already are operating a business, you may wish to have your current business documents (charter, operational, contracts) reviewed, for relevancy and accuracy, by an attorney who is familiar with equine activities.

Remember the devil is in the details and the best way to stay organized is with the assistance of your own "business team" of professionals. Interview two or three professionals and look for an individual who is knowledgeable, skilled, and communicates well with you. Building your business for success will be easier when you're surrounded by expertise.

CHAPTER 14

Speciality Areas

*"Maryland is rich with a variety of breeds and disciplines.
Know which governing agency oversees your
particular discipline."*

Legal concerns with horses often depend on the type of horse and the use of the horse. If the horse is a racer, a show or competitive sport horse, or used in organized recreational endeavors, there will be issues of registry and licensing, drug and medication use, and competitive rules and regulations. It is advisable to keep current with the particular rules and regulations of the governing association.

For competitive showing, horse owners, trainers, and riders must be members of the United States Equestrian Federation (USEF). This is the regulatory agency for the various breeds and disciplines involved in competitive horse shows and exhibitions. The USEF is the rule-maker and enforcer for those events sanctioned by them. In the event of a violation (rule or drug-use), the USEF conducts its own administrative hearings.

Thoroughbreds, Standardbreds, Arabians, and Quarter Horses are breeds used for breed-specific racing. Other breeds may be used in steeplechase racing as well. Maryland recognizes steeplechases, flat-track races (Thoroughbreds), and Standardbred racing (trotters and pacers). The Jockey Club oversees all thoroughbred racing and establishes the national rules and regulations for racing thoroughbreds. The U.S. Trotting Association oversees the national rules and regulations of trotters and pacers. In Maryland, the Maryland Racing Commission is the regulatory agency for all racing breeds. Violations of rules and drug-use are adjudicated first through the Maryland Racing Commission. Appeals of MRC rulings may be brought into the Maryland courts.

Other equine-related activities with their own discipline or breed-specific rules and regulations include Jousting, Polo, Competitive Trail events, Hunt Clubs, Rodeo events (i.e. penning, roping, reining), Long-Distance Trail or Endurance Rides, and 4-H activities. By and far, the majority of horses in Maryland are used for individual sport and pleasure activities. The 2010 Maryland Equine Census[1] commissioned by the Maryland Horse Industry Board summarized the total number of equine reported in the state to be about 80,000. Almost 49% of the horses in Maryland are used for purposes other than racing.

The largest population of horses (excluding racing stables) are found in Baltimore, Montgomery, Frederick, and Prince George's counties. Although the horse, whether an athlete or someone's backyard companion, can be found in every county of Maryland.

The benefits of horses in the State of Maryland exceeds the personal satisfaction one derives from owning, riding, or working with the equine. Society also benefits from the jobs generated to support this vast industry with its varied disciplines and events. Thousands of dollars are spent annually on equipment, tack, supplies, feed, farrier, dental and veterinarian care, special services (such as massage, chiropractic, and acupuncture), land, and buildings. The horse industry continues to be a very substantive commodity in Maryland.

Whichever breed or discipline you choose to become involved, remember an attorney with good "horse sense" can help you through the good times and bad times of horse ownership. Long live the equine industry in Maryland!

Sample Of Customized Contracts
And Legal Forms For Equine Operations

Business Entities

- Limited Liability Company • Corporation • Joint Ventures and General Partnerships
- Syndications • Family Farms

Work / Employment Contracts

- Independent Contractors • Employees • Volunteers

Participant Agreement (Liability Waiver and Hold Harmless Agreement)

- Helmet Waiver (optional – not recommended)

Rules & Regulations (of facility)

Price and Fee Schedule (of facility)

Boarding Agreements (full service and self care)

- Application forms (reference checks) • Full Board • Field Board

Training and Lesson Agreements

- Student Lessons • Equine Training

Horse Information Form

Rider Information Form

Lease Agreements (Horse)

- Full Lease • Half Lease • Lease to Own

Other Lease Agreements (Equipment; stables; pastures; housing, etc)

Purchase and Sale Agreements

- Cash Sale • Installment Sale - with or without Trial Period • Bill of Sale
- Promissory Note

Consignment and Agency Agreements (limited POA)

Breeding Contacts

- Live Cover or Artificial Insemination (AI) • Breeding Agreement / Foal Exchange
- Certificate of Breeding • Agreement for Lease of Mare
- Stallion Lease Agreement • Agreement of Sale of Unborn Foal

OTHER CUSTOMIZED CONTRACTS AND FORMS FOR SPECIFIC NEEDS AND CIRCUMSTANCES.

EVERYTHING IN WRITING!

START WITH YOUR LIABILITY RELEASE FORM

SALE OF HORSE

(I) Consignment Agreement with Owner of Horse
1) Consignment agreement with owner (agency/lpoa)
2) Advertising*
3) Contract with prospective buyer
   a) Sales & Purchase Agreement (cash); or
   b) S & P Agreement (installment); or
   c) Pre-purchase Trial Agreement; or
   d) Lease w/Option to Buy Agreement
4) Bill of Sale (transfer of registration papers *if applicable*)

or

(II) Purchase from private sale / auction
1) Sales & Purchase Contract with owner / auction house
2) Bill of Sale (registration papers)
3) Advertising*
4) Contract with prospective buyer
   a) Sales & Purchase Agreement (cash); or
   b) S & P Agreement (installment); or
   c) Pre-purchase Trial Agreement; or
   d) Lease w/Option to Buy Agreement
5) Bill of Sale (transfer of registration papers *if applicable*)

or

(III) Personally owned horse
1) Advertising*
2) Contract with prospective buyer
   a) Sales & Purchase Agreement (cash); or
   b) S & P Agreement (installment); or
   c) Pre-purchase Trial Agreement; or
   d) Lease w/Option to Buy Agreement
3) Bill of Sale (transfer of registration papers *if applicable*)

LEASING OF HORSE

(I) Horse owned by other
1) Agreement w/owner to lease out horse
2) Lease agreement w/Lessee
   a) Full Lease; or
   b) Partial or Limited Use Lease; or
   c) Lease w/Option to Buy; or
   d) Free Lease

or

(II) Personally owned horse
1) Lease agreement w/Lessee
   a) Full Lease; or
   b) Partial or Limited Use Lease; or
   c) Lease w/Option to Buy; or
   d) Free Lease

BREEDING

(I) Broodmare Lease
(II) Stallion Service Agreement
   a) Live Cover
   b) A.I.
(III) Foal Sharing Contracts

BOARDING AND TRAINING OF HORSE

(I) Boarding Agreement w/Owner (horse info form)
   a) Full Board w/stall or Field Board
   b) Self Board
   c) Owner/Rider information sheet
(II) Training Agreement w/Owner
   a) included w/boarding agreement
   b) seperate agreement

LESSONS

(I) Lesson Agreement w/rider
   (rider info form)

LEASING FACILITY

(I) Full Lease of Facility [landlord/tenant]
(II) Limited Lease for Equine Activities
   a) Pony & Horse Clubs
   b) Community Groups

STAFFING AGREEMENTS

1) Trainers
   a) Employee **
   b) Independent Contractor
2) Stable Staff
   a) Employee **
   b) Bartering
   c) Volunteers
3) Administrative Assistance
   a) Employee **
   b) Contractual
   c) Bartering
   d) Volunteers

HOUSING / TENANT AGREEMENTS

Check individual county code for licensing requirements for tenant housing

* Representations made in advertisements can become a liability issue.
** IRS criteria determine difference between employee and independent contractor. Employees may be full time, part time, casual, or seasonal. But determining status is extremely important for workers compensation, employment tax requirements, and other liability issues.

Business Plan Outline

COVER PAGE
-Name of Business
-Contact Information
-Date

FIRST PAGE
- Table of Contents

FOLLOWING PAGES
(1) Executive Summary
- Name of Business
- Contact Person
- Other Persons/companies involved with business operations
- Describe business and related products/services

(2) Targeted market(s)

(3) Stage of development business is in currently

(4) Evaluation of risks involved, what potential profit

(5) Business Mission Statement

(6) Market Analysis

(7) Key Success Factors (Summary)
- strength of business
- management team (what experience, talents, education, training)
- reputation in the industry
- contacts in the industry

(8) Vision of the business (what the company will be in the future)
- financial
- personalized services

(9) Milestones (event and target date)
- financing arranged
- building completed
- enlarging/adding to facilities completed
- hiring for business opening completed
- advertising/promotion begins (i.e. website, marketing)
- service begins

(10) Financing Statements/Projections

(11) Exhibits
- Resumes of Key Personnel
- Promotional materials
- Related market information

Articles of Organization
of
Name of Company

The undersigned, with the intention of creating a Maryland Limited Liability Company files the following Articles of Organization:

(1) NAME: (must include "LLC", "L.L.C.", "Limited Liability Company" as part of the name) The name of the Limited Liability Company is _____

(2) PURPOSES: (Should enumerate activities current and possible activities in the future for which the LLC will operate.) The purpose for which the Company is filed, includes, but is not limited to, as follows:

    (a)_____;
    (b)_____;
    (c)_____; and
    (d) And for any lawful act or activity for which limited liability companies may be organized in the State of Maryland.

(3) COMPANY ADRESS: (Primary location or business office location. NO P.O. Box addresses. Address must include Street, City, State, and Zip Code.) The address of the Company is_____
_____

(4) RESIDENT AGENT LANGUAGE: (Must be at least 18 yrs of age, resident of Maryland; may also be a "resident agent company" – but not very cost effective. Incorporator may also serve as own resident agent.)The resident agent is…(Name of resident agent)_____ whose address is (address of resident agent)_____

(5) OPERATIONAL LANGUAGE: (Note: If this language is not used, all operational procedures of LLC default to the provisions contained in Maryland Limited Liability Act). Pursuant to §4A-402 of the Maryland Limited Liability Act, the Company shall regulate and establish its operational procedures through an Operating Agreement.

(6) AGENCY LANGUAGE (three choices): Pursuant to §4A-401(a)(3) of the Maryland Limited Liability Company Act, no member of the Company shall be an agent of the Company solely by virtue of being a member, and no member shall have authority to act for **the Company solely by virtue of being a member.**
OR Pursuant to §4A-401 of the Maryland Limited Liability Act, the Company recognizes for the purposes of conducting and operating the Company the authorized agents to be (<u>names of incorporators</u>).
OR Pursuant to §4A-401 of the Maryland Limited Liability Act, the Company recognizes for the purposes of conducting and operating the Company the sole authorized agent to be (<u>name of incorporator</u>).

NOTE:
Also need (1) Signature Block (include all incorporators' signatures), date signed; and (2) Resident Agent acceptance and acknowledgment language with signature and date. Try and keep the Articles to one page if possible, SDAT charges for each page, not as one document. In the lower left hand corner note the address where certified copies are to be returned. Certified copies returned to law office; copy made and original certified copy(ies) returned to incorporators. Certified copy should be safeguarded in company's records. Banks often required a certified copy of Articles for the purpose of opening bank accounts.

Articles of Incorporation
For a Stock Corporation

FIRST: The undersigned, _____, whose address is/are _____ _____, being at least eighteen (18) years of age, do(es) hereby form a corporation under the laws of the State of Maryland.

SECOND: The name of the corporation is _____.

THIRD: The purpose(s) for which the corporation is formed is/are as   follows:

FOURTH: The street address of the principal office of the corporation in Maryland is:

FIFTH: The name of the resident agent of the corporation in Maryland is (name and address):

SIXTH: The corporation has authority to issue _____shares at $_____par value per share.

SEVENTH: The number of directors of the corporation shall be   which number may be increased or decreased pursuant to the Bylaws of the corporation. The name(s) of the director(s) who shall act until the first meeting or until their successors are dully chosen and qualified is/are:

IN WITNESS WHEREOF, I have signed these articles and acknowledge the same to be my act:

Signature Block of Incorporator(s):

I hereby consent to my designation in this document as Resident Agent for this corporation:

Signature Block of Resident Agent as name in Fifth paragraph.

Filing Party's Name and Return Address

Articles of Incorporation
For A Close Corporation

FIRST: The undersigned, _____, whose address is/are,_____
_____being at least eighteen (18) years of age, do(es) hereby form a corporation under the laws of the State of Maryland. The corporation shall be a close corporation.

SECOND: The name of the corporation is _____.

THIRD: The purpose(s) for which the corporation is formed is/are as follows:

FOURTH: The street address of the principal office of the corporation in Maryland is:

FIFTH: The name of the resident agent of the corporation in Maryland is (name and address):

SIXTH: The corporation has authority to issue _____shares at $_____par value per share.

SEVENTH: The corporation elects to have no board of directors. Until such election takes effect _____will be the director.

IN WITNESS WHEREOF, I have signed these articles and acknowledge the same to be my act:

Signature Block of Incorporator(s):

I hereby consent to my designation in this document as Resident Agent for this corporation:

Signature Block of Resident Agent as name in Fifth paragraph.

Filing Party's Name and Return Address

Articles Of Incorporation
For A Nonstock Corporation

FIRST: The undersigned, _____, whose address is/are _____ _____, being at least eighteen (18) years of age, do(es) hereby form a corporation under the laws of the State of Maryland.

SECOND: The name of the corporation is _____.

THIRD: The purpose(s) for which the corporation is formed is/are as follows: _____.

FOURTH: The street address of the principal office of the corporation in Maryland is:

FIFTH: The name of the resident agent of the corporation in Maryland is (name and address):

SEVENTH: The number of directors of the corporation shall be_____which number may be increased or decreased pursuant to the Bylaws of the corporation. The name(s) of the director(s) who shall act until the first meeting or until their successors are dully chosen and qualified is/are:

IN WITNESS WHEREOF, I have signed these articles and acknowledge the same to be my act:

Signature Block of Incorporator(s):

I hereby consent to my designation in this document as Resident Agent for this corporation:

Signature Block of Resident Agent as name in Fifth paragraph.

Filing Party's Name and Return Address

Articles Of Incorporation
For A Tax-Exempt Nonstock Corporation

FIRST: The undersigned, _____, whose address is/are _____
_____, being at least eighteen (18) years of age, do(es) hereby form a corporation under the laws of the State of Maryland.

SECOND: The name of the corporation is _____.

THIRD: The purpose(s) for which the corporation is formed is/are as follows:_____.
Said corporation is organized exclusively for charitable, religious, educational, and/or scientific purposes, including, for such purposes, the making of distributions to organizations that qualify as exempt organizations under Section 501(c)(3) of the Internal Revenude Code, or the corresponding section of any future federal tax code.

FOURTH: The street address of the principal office of the corporation in Maryland is:

FIFTH: The name of the resident agent of the corporation in Maryland is (name and address):

SIXTH: The corporation has no authority to issue capital stock.

SEVENTH: The number of directors of the corporation shall be___which number may be increased or decreased pursuant to the Bylaws of the corporation. The name(s) of the director(s) who shall act until the first meeting or until their successors are dully chosen and qualified is/are:

EIGHTH: No part of the net earnings of the corporation shall inure to the benefit of, or be distributable to its members, trustees, officers, or other private persons, except that the corporation shall be authorized and empowered to pay reasonable compensation for services rendered and to make payments and distributions in furtherance of the purposes set forth in Article Third hereof. No substantial part of the activities of the corporation shall be the carrying on of propaganda, or otherwise attempting to influence legislation, and the corporation shall not participate in, or intervene in (including the publishing or distribution of statements) any political campaign on behalf of or in opposition to any candidate for public office. Notwithstanding any other provision of these articles, the corporation shall not carry on any other activities not permitted to be carried on (a) by a corporation exempt from federal income tax under Section 501(c)(3) of the Internal Revenue Code, or the corresponding section of any future federal tax code, or (b) by a corporation, contributions to which are deductible under Section 170(c)(2) of the Internal Revenue Code, or the corresponding section of any future federal tax code.

NINTH: Upon the dissolution of the corporation, assets shall be distributed for one or more exempt purposes within the meaning of Section 501(c)(3) of the Internal Revenue Code, or the corresponding section of any future federal tax code, or shall be distributed to the federal government, or to a state or local government, for a public purpose. Any such assets not so disposed of shall be disposed of by a Court of Competent Jurisdiction of the county in which the principal office of the corporation is then located, exclusively for such purposes or to such organization or organizations, as said Court shall determine, which are organized and operated exclusively for such purposes.

IN WITNESS WHEREOF, I have signed these articles and acknowledge the same to be my act:

Signature Block of Incorporator(s):

I hereby consent to my designation in this document as Resident Agent for this corporation:

Signature Block of Resident Agent as name in Fifth paragraph.

Filing Party's Name and Return Address

Client Checklist for a General Partnership

A. FORMATION DATA

1. **Name of Partnership:** _____
   Trade Name (if applicable):_____

2. **Address and Telephone Numbers of Partnership** (office):

3. **Resident Agent for Service of Process** (name and address):

4. **Nature of Partnership Business:** (describe)

5. **Ownership of Real Property** If there is ownership of real property, describe: _____

6. **Partners** (Name, Home & Business Addresses, Phone Number, Social Security Number)

7. **Capital Contributions** (Name, Percent Contribution (Money, Services, etc.)
   (1) Name_____
   %_____Describe contribution _____
   _____

8. **Percentage Allocations of Income and Loss** (Name and Percentage Interest for Each Partner):

9. **Special Allocations** (Distributions different from standard percentage arrangement): ____

10. **Name and Address of Bank:** _____

11. **Preparation of SS-4 Form (EIN)** ❑ Yes   ❑ No
    Prepared by: _____
    a. Fiscal Year:_____
    b. Peak number of employees expected during first twelve months:_____
    c. First date wages will be paid:_____
    d. Nature of business: _____
    e. Description of products or services: _____
    f. If filing by fax, is power of attorney complete? ❑ Yes   ❑ No

12. **Preparation for application for state tax I.D., if applicable:**   ❑ Yes   ❑ No
    Prepared by: _____

B.   NAMES, ADDRESSES, TELEPHONE, AND FAX NUMBERS OF KEY PEOPLE

13.   Accountant:

Name, Company Name, Address, Phone Numbers

14.   Insurance Agent:

Name, Company Name, Address, Phone Numbers

15.   Banker:

Name, Company Name, Address, Phone Numbers

16.   Attorney:

Name, Company Name, Address, Phone Numbers

17.   Partner(s) who will primarily work with attorney:

C.   MANAGEMENT AND BUSINESS OPERATIONS: (describe business operations; which partners are responsible for specific management of operations, etc.):

Client Checklist for a Limited Partnership

A.   FORMATION DATA

1.   **Name of Partnership:** _____

     Trade Name (if applicable):_____

2.   **Address and Telephone Numbers of Partnership** (office):

3.   **Resident Agent for Service of Process** (name and address):

4.   **Nature of Partnership Business:** (describe)

5.   **Ownership of Real Property** (If there is ownership of real property, describe)

6.   **General Partners** (Name, Home & Business Addresses, Phone Number, Social Security Number(s))

7.   **Limited Partners** (Name, Home & Business Addresses, Phone Number, Social Security Number(s))

8.   **Capital Contributions** (Name, Percent Contribution (Money, Services, etc.)

     (1) Name_____

     % _____ Describe contribution _____

9.   **Percentage Allocations of Income and Loss** (Name and Percentage Interest)

10.   **Special Allocations** (Distributions different from standard percentage arrangement)

11.   **Name and Address of Bank**

12.   **Preparation of SS-4 Form (EIN)** ❑ Yes   ❑ No

     Prepared by: _____

     a.   Fiscal Year:_____

     b.   Peak number of employees expected during first twelve months:_____

     c.   First date wages will be paid:_____

     d.   Nature of business: _____

     e.   Description of products or services:_____

     f.   If filing by fax, is power of attorney complete?   ❑ Yes   ❑ No

13.   **Preparation for application for state tax I.D., if applicable:** ❑ Yes   ❑ No

Prepared by: _____

B.   NAMES, ADDRESSES, TELEPHONE, AND FAX NUMBERS OF KEY PEOPLE

14.   Accountant: (Name, Company, Address, Phone Numbers)

15.   Insurance Agent: (Name, Company, Address, Phone Numbers)

16   Banker: (Name, Company, Address, Phone Numbers)

C.   NOTES

17.   Partner(s) which will primarily work with attorney:

OPERATING AGREEMENT
of
(company name)

This Operating Agreement ("Agreement") of the _____(company name)_____, a Maryland (type   of business entity)___ ("Company"), dated as of (date of   execution)__ , is entered into by _____ (name/s),_____(address, city, state, zip)_____ and the Company (or other names) (collectively known as the "Parties").

Explanatory Statement

The Parties have agreed to organize and operate the Company in accordance with the terms of, and subject to the conditions set forth in, this Agreement.

NOW, THEREFORE, for good and valuable consideration, the Parties, intending to be legally bound, agree as follows:

Section I
Defined Terms

Capitalized words and phrases used and not otherwise defined elsewhere in this Agreement have the following meanings:

1.1 **"Act"** means the Maryland Limited Liability Company Act [**or other appropriate business entity formation**], as amended from time to time.[1]

1.2 **"Articles of Organization"** means the Articles of Organization of the Company filed with SDAT on _____(date of filing)_____.[2] (May also be referred to as the "charter document.")

1.3 **"Capital Account"** means the account maintained by the Company for each Interest Holder in accordance with the following provisions:

(i) An Interest Holder's Capital Account shall be credited with the Interest Holder's Capital Contributions, the amount of any Company liabilities assumed by the Interest Holder (or which are secured by Company property distributed to the Interest Holder), the Interest Holder's allocable share of Profit; and

(ii) An Interest Holder's Capital Account shall be debited with the amount of money and the fair market value of any Company property distributed to the Interest Holder, the amount of any liabilities of the Interest Holder assumed by the Company and the Interest Holder's allocable share of Loss.

If any Interest is transferred pursuant to the terms of this Agreement, the Transferee shall succeed to the Capital Account of the Transferor to the extent the Capital Account is attributable to the transferred Interest. Notwithstanding any provision of this Agreement to the contrary, each Interest Holder's Capital Account shall be maintained and adjusted in accordance with the Regulations, including, without limitation (i) the adjustments permitted or required by Code Section 704(b) and, to the extent applicable, the principles expressed in Code

Section 704(c), and (ii) adjustments required to maintain Capital Accounts in accordance with the "substantial economic effect test" set forth in Code Section 704(b).

1.4 **"Capital Contribution"** means the total amount of cash and fair market value (net of liabilities assumed or taken subject to by the Company) of any other assets contributed (or deemed contributed under Treasury Regulations Section 1.704.1) to the Company by a Member.

1.5 **"Cash Flow"** means all cash funds derived from operations of the Company (including interest received on reserves), without reduction for any non-cash charges, but less cash funds used to pay current operating expenses and to pay or establish reasonable reserves for future expenses, debt payments, capital improvements, and replacements as determined by the Members. Cash Flow shall be increased by the reduction of any reserve previously established.

1.6 **"Code"** means the Internal Revenue Code of 1985, as amended, or any corresponding provision of any succeeding law.

1.7 **"Interest"** means a Person's share of the Profits and Losses of, and the right to receive distributions from, the Company.

1.8 **"Interest Holder"** means any Person who holds an Interest, whether as a Member or as an unadmitted assignee of a Member.

1.9 **"Member"** means each Person signing this Agreement and any Person who subsequently is admitted as a Member of the Company pursuant to this Agreement.

1.10 "Membership Rights" means all the rights of a Member in the Company, including a Member's: (i) Interest, (ii) right to inspect the Company's books and records, and (iii) right to participate in the management of and vote on matters coming before the Company as set forth in Section V of this Agreement.

1.11 "Negative Capital Account" means a Capital Account with a balance of less than zero.

1.12 "Ordinary Course of Business" means that which is normally done in managing and operating a business in the same or similar industry, included but not limited to, the power to execute for and on behalf of the company any and all documents and instruments. Under no circumstances will any transaction involving amounts greater than <u>(fill in written and numerical amount)</u> be considered within the ordinary course of business.

1.13 "Percentage" means, as to a Member, the Percentage set forth after the Member's name on Exhibit A to this Agreement, as amended from time to time, and as to an Interest Holder who is not a Member, the Percentage of the Member whose Interest has been acquired by such Interest Holder, to the extent the Interest Holder has succeeded to that Member's Interest.

1.14 "Person" means and includes an individual, corporation, partnership, association, limited liability company, trust, estate, or other entity.

1.15 "Positive Capital Account" means a Capital Account with a balance greater than zero.

1.16 "Profit and Loss" means for each taxable year of the Company (or other period for which Profit and Loss must be computed), the Company's taxable income or loss determined in accordance with Code Section 703, by the Company in consultation with its accountant.

1.17 "Regulations" means the income tax regulations of the Treasury Department, including any temporary regulations, promulgated from time to time pursuant to the Code.

1.18 "SDAT" means the State Department of Assessments and Taxation of Maryland.

1.19 "Transfer" means, when used as a noun, any voluntary sale, hypothecation,[3] pledge, assignment, attachment, or other transfer, and, when used as a verb, means voluntarily to sell, hypothecate, pledge, assign, or otherwise turn over to another Person.

1.20 "Voluntary Withdrawal" means a Member's disassociation with the Company.

Section II
Formation and Name; Office; Purpose; Term

2.1   Organization. _____(date of filing).

2.2   Name of the Company. _____(name of company).

2.3   Purpose. The Company is organized for the purposes stated in the Articles of Organization.

2.4   Term. The term of the Company began upon the execution of this Agreement and shall continue until its existence is terminated pursuant to Section VII of the Agreement.

2.5   Principal Office. The principal office of the Company is stated in the Articles of Organization.

2.6   Resident Agent. The name and address of the Company's resident agent in the State of Maryland are stated in the Articles of Organization.

2.7   Members. The name, present mailing address, taxpayer identification number, and Percentage of each Member are set forth on Exhibit A to this Agreement.

Section III
Members; Capital; Capital Accounts

3.1   Initial Capital Contributions. (provision when full initial capital contribution must be made – typically w/in 6 months – see Exhibit A)

3.2   Additional Issuance of Interest. (option to include other Interest Holders)

3.3   No Other Capital Contributions Required. (no additional capital required beyond initial contribution)

3.4   No Interest on Capital Contributions. Interest Holders shall not be paid interest on their Capital Contributions.

3.5   Return of Capital Contributions. Except as otherwise provided in this Agreement, no Interest Holder shall have the right to withdraw or receive any return of any Capital Contribution made by that Interest Holder.

3.6   Form of Return of Capital. (returns to Members may be in cash, notes, property, or a combination)

3.7   Capital Accounts. (separate Capital Accounts for each Member)

3.8   Loans. (only upon approval of all Members may a Member incur a loan for the Company)

Section IV
Profit, Loss, and Distribution

4.1   Distribution of Cash Flow. Cash Flow for each taxable year of the Company shall be distributed to the Interest Holders in proportion to their Percentages **no later than seventy-five (75) days after the end of the taxable year OR other method of distribution – may opt to distribute only if certain percentage of profit is realized, or only upon dissolution of Company.**...

4.2   Allocation of Profit or Loss. (in proportion to percentage of ownership)

4.3   Allocation of Tax Items. (same distribution/percentage of tax liability as profit and loss allocation)

4.4   Liquidation and Dissolution. Liquidation and Dissolution of the assets of the Company shall be conducted in accordance with the following provisions:

4.4.1 (method of distribution of assets to Members if Company dissolved)

4.4.2 No Interest Holder shall be obligated to restore a Negative Capital Account.

4.5 General Provisions.

4.5.1 Except as otherwise provided in this Agreement, the timing and amount of all distributions shall be determined by the Members.

4.5.2 (fair market value of Company assets)

4.5.3 (how profits and losses are allocated)

4.5.4 It is the intention of the Member that the Company shall be taxed   choice   of "sole proprietor," "partnership," or "corporation."

Section V
Management: Rights, Powers, and Duties

5.1   Management. (provision how Company is managed; may denote "Members," a "Director" or "Manager" supervise by the Members and/or President of the Company.)

5.2   Meetings and Voting by Members. The conduct of business meetings and voting activities shall be in accordance with the following provisions:

5.21. Meetings:_____**(how often)**_____
_____

Voting by person and/or proxy ?_____**(yes/no)**_____

5.2.2 Except as otherwise provided in this Agreement, the affirmative vote of the Members holding____what PERCENTAGE? (e.g. 50%) for approving matters...

5.2.3 Hold meetings by means of **telephone conference or similar communications equipment**_____**(yes/no)**

5.3   Personal Services. No Member shall be required to perform services for the Company solely by virtue of being a Member. Unless approved by the Members, no Member shall perform services or incur expenses in connection with activities of the Company.

5.4   Officers. Options include (1) no officers or (2) at a minimum, President, Secretary, and Treasurer.

Choices: _____
_____
_____

5.5   Indemnification. (and other options include: D&O Insurance; Professional Insurance; Business Liability; etc. – as applicable)

Section VI
Transfer of Interests and Withdrawal of Members

6.1 Transfers. No Member or other Interest Holder may transfer all, or any portion of, or any interest or rights in the Interest owned by that Member or Interest Holder **CHOICES: (1) except upon the death of that Member or Interest Holder; OR (2) upon the death of the Member or Interest Holder all Interest and Membership Rights shall be transferred to the remaining Members of the Company. Interest may not be transferred, assigned, testated or otherwise passed to any Persons other than the Members of the Company. Such Interest shall be equally distributed to the remaining Members. All Members are hereby in agreement that this is their intent and do willfully and voluntarily consent to the above provision.**

6.2 Right of First Refusal. (provision providing proceeding for selling the Interest to the other Members and to third parties) permits a Member to "quit" the Company.

6.3 Third Party Transferee. Upon the Transfer of any Membership Interest to a third party pursuant to Section 6.2, the Transferee shall become an Interest Holder in the Company.

6.4 Voluntary Withdrawal. No Member shall have the right or power to Voluntarily Withdrawal from the Company except as provided in Sections 6.2 and 6.3.

Section VII
Dissolution, Liquidation, and Termination of the Company

7.1 Events of Dissolution. The Company may be dissolved upon the unanimous written agreement of the Members. (also, involuntary dissolution – court order, bankruptcy, death of Member(s).)

7.2 Procedure for Winding Up and Dissolution. (method of paying off debts and then distribution of remaining money to Members)

7.3 Filing of Articles of Cancellation.[4] (provision detailing who is responsible for winding up business affairs: (1) remaining Members; (2) last Person; or (3) Legal or personal representatives of last Person.)

Section VIII
Books, Records, Accounting and Tax Elections

8.1 Bank Accounts. (generic language)
8.2 Books and Records. (generic language)
8.3 Annual Accounting Period. The annual accounting period of the Company shall be its taxable year. The Company's taxable year shall _____.

Section IX
General Provisions

9.1 Assurances. (provision detailing that the Members promise / assure that filing of documents as required by law will be done)

9.2 Notifications. (provision on the manner in which Members receive notices)

9.3   Specific Performances. (provision detailing right for specific performance for breach or anticipated breach of Agreement)

9.4   Complete Agreement. (provision that this is THE Agreement – supersedes all other oral or written agreements.)

9.5   Binding Provisions. (provision that this binds Members and all heirs, etc)

9.6   Separability Provisions. (if any one provision found invalid by law, whole Agreement is not invalid.)

9.7   Counterparts. (one or more counterparts may be execute and considered original and whole to Agreement)

9.8   Applicable Law. (Maryland law applies)

9.9   Mediation of Disputes. (first mediation before litigation)

9.10 Jurisdiction and Venue. (Maryland state or federal courts)

9.11 Section Titles. (convenience for reading, not defining)

9.12 Terms. (common nouns and pronouns)

   IN WITNESS WHEREOF, the Parties have executed, or caused this Agreement to be executed, as of the date set forth herein above.

MEMBER(S):

_____

(name)
(title)

_____

(name)
(title)

EXHIBIT A
TO OPERATING AGREEMENT OF
(company name)
EIN _____

Member Name and Address	Social Security Number	Capital Contribution	Percentage Interest
Name Street City, State, Zip Code	#	$	%
Name Street City, State, Zip Code	#	$	%

Bylaws

NOTES:
- ✓   Customize Bylaws according to the particular needs of the organization.
- ✓   Use subheadings within Articles to distinguish topics.
- ✓   Bold headings and subheadings for ease of reading.

ARTICLE I – ASSOCIATION / CORPORATION NAME

ARTICLE II - OFFICE
1. Location
2. Other locations (if applicable)

ARTICLE III – PURPOSES OF ORGANIZATION
(List particular purposes and methods of activities)

ARTICLE IV – FISCAL YEAR
The fiscal year of the Corporation shall begin _____ and end _____ each year.

ARTICLE V – MEMBERSHIP (if applicable)
1. Qualifications of membership ("member in good standing")
2. Category of memberships
3. Assignment of voting rights of members

ARTICLE VI – BOARD OF DIRECTORS
1. General Powers
2. Number and Term of Office
3. Nomination and Election of Directors
4. Filling of Vacancies
5. Compensation of Directors

ARTICLE VII – OFFICERS
1. Number and Tenure of Officers
2. Nominations and Election of Officers
3. Filling of Vacancies
4. Compensation of Officers
5. President – Powers and Duties
6. Vice President – Powers and Duties
7. Secretary – Powers and Duties
8. Treasurer – Powers and Duties

ARTICLE VIII – RIGHTS AND DUTIES OF DIRECTORS AND OFFICERS
1. General Definition of Duties
2. Duty of Care
    i. Definition
    ii. Responsibilities
        a) Meeting attendance
        b) Communication
        c) Delegation
3) Duty of Loyalty
    i. Definition
    ii. Responsibilities
        a) Confidentiality
        b) Corporate Opportunity
        c) Conflict of Interest

4) Rights
    i. Management Access
    ii. Books and Records
    iii. Notice of Meetings
    iv. Right to Dissent
    v. Minutes

ARTICLE IX – INDEMNIFICATION
1. Definition (§ 2-418 MD Corps & Assocs)
2. Indemnification of Directors and Officers
3. Indemnification of Employees and Agents (including Volunteers)

ARTICLE X – MEETINGS
1. Annual Meeting
    a. Board of Directors
    b. Members (if applicable)
2. Regular Meetings
    a. Board of Directors
    b. Members (if applicable)
3. Special Meetings
    a. Purpose
    b. Method of calling a special meeting
4. Notice of Meetings
    a. Method
5. Quorum (required to conduct a business meeting)
6. Voting (required to pass resolutions)

ARTICLE XI – VOTING
1. Method of Voting (i.e., paper ballot, hand count, voice count)
2. Nomination Procedure for Election

ARTICLE XIII – POLITICAL ACTIVITIES
1. Corporation is authorized / not authorized to

    a. Public policy issues (permissible activities for nonprofits i.e., conduct educational meetings; voter registration drives)

    b. Lobbying activities (i.e., influence legislation)

    c. Candidate contributions

ARTICLE XIV – COMMITTEES (if applicable)

ARTICLE XV - AMENDMENTS
The Board of Directors shall have the power and authority to amend, alter, or repeal these Bylaws or any provision as deemed necessary from time to time.

Components Of "Waiver Of Liability - Hold Harmless Agreement"

A "Waiver of Liability" or "Hold Harmless Agreement" needs to be clearly written and understandable to those individuals agreeing to waive certain legal rights. Maryland recognizes waivers of liability, but will scrutinize the language for unreasonable or voidable agreements. Parents cannot waive the rights of their minor child, but by signing the Agreement on behalf of their child (as well as having the minor read and sign) puts the parent on notice that the activities upon which their minor child are to engage are considered high-risk. Maryland is also unique in that it embraces the concept of contributory negligence, rather than comparative negligence. This is advantageous to the equine facility operator, although not so favorable to the negligent participant.

I have designed such agreements with the following eight components:

1) **Title:** I typically title my waivers as a "Participant Agreement" as it is an all-encompassing assumption of risk, waiver of liability, and indemnification agreement. My agreements are two-pages and are designed to be signed by participants of legal age and also by minors along with parental signature.

2) **Assumption of Inherent Risks:** this is a statement that requires the participant to acknowledge the inherent risks (up to including death) of equine activities.

3) **Waiver of Liability:** this is a statement by which the participant agrees to waive liability against the facility resulting from ordinary (active or passive) negligence of facility. One can never waive liability resulting from gross (willful and intentional) negligence.

4) **Indemnification:** a statement that the participant will hold harmless, defend, and indemnify the facility due to participants' actions. Participant accepts the risks of reimbursing facility or third parties due to participant's conduct.

5) **Acknowledgements, Assertions and Agreements:** these statements require the participant to provide a full and fair disclosure of their equestrian experiences/abilities/skills and contains additional statements relative to "Health Status," "Emergency Care," and "Rules & Safety Equipment."

6) **Covenant not to Sue; Mediation; Venue; and Severability Clauses:** this section contains statements which the participant agrees not to sue the facility for any present or future claims based on the active or passive negligence of the facility. Specifies venue in the State of Maryland, as well as agreement to mediate prior to taking litigious action.

7) **Acknowledgement of Understanding:** this section is bolded and set apart at the end of the Agreement as it states the participant has read the two-pages, fully understand its terms, and voluntarily agrees to the terms and conditions.

8) **Date and Signature lines, along with complete contact information.** Although a parent cannot waive their child's rights, by having both the child and parent sign it emphasizes to the minor the seriousness of this activity and it puts the parent on notice of the high risk activities they are allowing their child to participate. Complete contact information is essential in the case of emergencies or other situations whereby the facility needs to contact the individual.

STABLE NAME
Stable License
TOP TEN BARN RULES

#1 Children under the age of 16 must be supervised by a responsible adult at all times.

#2 Participants, Guests and Spectators must sign a release of liability form and observe posted safety rules. (You might even want to give a guided tour for first time visitors!).

#3 Be considerate of other participants and staff.

#4 Riders under age 18 must wear an ASTM/SEI approved helmet with chinstrap properly attached while riding.

#5 No smoking is allowed in the barn, lounge or riding arenas at any time.

#6 No dogs or other pets allowed on the premises (or must be leashed/restrained at all times)

#7 No running, rough-housing, shouting, or throwing things on the premises.

#8 All riders must wear safe footgear when working around horses.

#9 Practice safe horse handling at all times.

#10 No alcohol, illegal drugs, or weapons on premises.

Although these are basic rules for most barns, Barn Rules and Regulations should be specific to your type of facility and equine operations. Through consultation and observation, customized Rules & Regulations are developed for your barn operations. Don't trust that a rider coming to your facility is already safety minded. Take the time to talk to them about safety and your "rules and regulations" at your facility!

A Release of Liability (or Hold Harmless Agreement) is vital to all equine facilities. State laws vary and are very specific as to the liability of high risk activities. Maryland does not have a specific equine liability statute. Consultation with an attorney will ensure your Release is legally binding (and not just a generic form downloaded off the Internet or one containing language non-specific to the State of Maryland or not pertinent to your facility).

Also consider adding a set of "consequences" to your barn rules. What measures will you take for a safe and fun environment? How will you handle the habitual violator? Will there be a time when you might need to enlist the help of local police enforcement? Talk with your attorney. Be certain your rules and consequences are fair and easy to enforce. It'll make time at the barn more fun!

Name of Stable
Boarding Agreement

THIS BOARDING AGREEMENT made by and between NAME   ("Stable"), and _____
_____("Owner"). Stable and Owner desire to enter
into this agreement upon the terms and conditions contained below and to be legally bound.

1. Location, Fees, and Terms.
(a) Location.
    Include physical address, County.
    Include statement: Any reference to premises of Stable shall be construed to include only the real
    property and buildings located at the address so noted and which is used for Stable's equine busi-
    ness and operation.
(b) Duration.
    Note if this is a month to month or a yearly contract.
    Note how and when agreement can be renewed.
(c) Boarding Fees.
    Need to notify owner of Stable's right to change fees. "Boarding fees are subject to change at
    Stable's discretion with thirty (30) days notice provided to Owner and shall not be construed as a
    material change to this agreement."
(d) Stall Boarding or Field BoardingFee.
    Note how much boarding is per horse per month.
    Note when payment is due.
    Note what is included with fee: (i.e. "Owner is given exclusive use of one stall per horse under this
    provision. Stall boarding also includes use and access to all pastures, trails, arena, run-in sheds,
    assigned storage areas and common areas of the barn, shared by the use of Stable or any other
    boarder.")
    Note if this is full care or self-care.
(e) Security Deposit.
    A security deposit is strongly suggested. Note how much the security deposit will be and when
    payment is required (at the time the boarding application was accepted, at the time of signing this
    agreement, prior to horse's arrival at farm, etc.)
    Include statement that the security deposit is held without liability of interest and the purpose is
    for security of performance by Owner. It is not an advance payment of boarding fees, nor a mea-
    sure of damages in the event of default. Also note how the funds are retained (separate account,
    commingled but accounted for, etc.) And when the security deposit will be returned (minus
    funds for damages, etc.)
(f) Late Fee.
    A late fee typically insures timely payment. Late fees can be charged on a daily basis, after a date
    certain – but cannot be excessive (i.e. cannot double regular boarding fee). Note here that if
    payment continues in arrears for thirty days or more the Stable shall exercise their right of the
    Maryland Livestock Lien (MD Comm Law, §16-401).
(g) Early Termination.
    Terms here can include the Stable's right to terminate the agreement if the horse is found danger-
    ous or undesireable to establishment, or for other reasons (named or unnamed) which the Stable
    may wish to terminate the agreement. Must also note how many days after termination notice
    when Owner must remove horse.
2. Description of Horse (NOTE: a separate boarding agreement must be completed for each indi-
    vidual horse.)
HORSE'S REGISTERED NAME: _____
"STABLE" or "BARN" NAME: _____
AGE: _____ FOALED (D.O.B.): _____GENDER: _____
COLOR & MARKINGS: _____
BREED: _____
REGISTRATION or TATTOO NO: _____
3. Ownership.
    Owner's representation that he/she is the owner – or if there are co-owners of the horse.

4. Feed, Facilities, Services and Property Storage.

Detailed description of services – whether self-care or full-care.

Note what standard services are included in the boarding fee (what the owner may be responsible such as blanketing, etc.)

Note if there are wash racks for use, or other similar facilities (i.e. laundry).

Note how Owner's property (tack trunk, etc.) may be stored. If the Owner is responsible for own lock, etc. AND note Stable is not liable for theft, loss, damage, or disappearance of any tack or equipment.

Note if trailer parking is available and if so, what the fees are (if applicable) – how spaces are assigned, etc.

5. Exercise and Other Services.

First note if this is Full or Self Care.

Note whether Owner is exclusively responsible for the horse's exercise or if training is part of the boarding agreement.

Note what other special (additional) services are available – should be noted on a "List of Services & Fee Schedule" and that the fees are subject to change at Stable's discretion.

6. Rules and Regulations.

The Owner should be acknowledging receipt of the "Rules & Regulations" – this should be a SEPARATE sheet also so Stable has more flexibility in changing or modifying the rules and regulations as necessary. Rules & Regulations should also be posted in the barn. A separate initial line here for Owner's acknowledgment of receipt.

7. General Health Care.

(a) Coggins Test. (Equine Infectious Anemia)

Note here that proof of a negative Coggins Test is required prior to delivery of the horse and annually thereafter.and that Owner is responsible for this test. Note if Stable has to render the services that Owner is financially obligated to pay the fee (plus any service charges) within x number of days after invoiced to Owner.

(b) Health Records and Services.

Note here that Owner is to provide health records of horse upon arrival and that the Owner is responsible for the ongoing health maintenance of the horse.

(c) Current Vaccinations.

Note that Owner is responsible for horse's ongoing vaccinations. Note what vaccinations are required, and which ones are recommended. (Required vaccinations: Rabies, Influenza, Rhino-pneumonitis, Tetanus Toxoid, West Niles Virus, and Eastern/Western/Venezuelan Equine Encephalitis. Recommended vaccinations: Strangles, Botulism.)

(d) Supplements and Worming.

Note here how supplements and the deworming program are administered (Owner, or Stable).

(e) Farrier Care.

Note here whether Owner or Stable arranges for farrier treatment. Also note that in the event Stable authorizes care due to Owner's neglect, the Owner is financial responsible for costs.

8. Emergency Care.

Important for Owner to provide contact information at all time – and what procedure Stable will take in the event of an emergency situation requiring medical treatment.

Also note that Owner is responsible for these costs, whether or not Stable successfully reached Owner prior to authorizing treatment.

A separate initial line should be included here whereby the Owner acknowledges if the horse is or is not a candidate for surgical care in the event of colic or other life-threatening illness.

9. Risk of Loss, Insurance and Disclosure.

(a) Risk of Loss.

Important to note that Stable is not responsible for sickness, disease, theft, estray, death or injury which may be suffered by the horseor for personal injury or disability.

(b) Insurance.

Note here whether or not Stable carries any insurance on horses not owned by Stable.

Note if Owner is required or encourage to carry insurance on the horse. If insurance exists, Owner must provide proof of policy.

(b) Disclosure of Horse's Traits and Behavior.

Important to have Owner acknowledge any traits or behavior of the horse (i.e. cribbing, biting, etc.) – this is usually found on the "Horse Information Form" and should be kept on file with a copy of this agreement. In the event these traits are discovered AFTER the horse becomes a boarder, Stable should notify the Owner of what is occurring – particularly if it is causing damage to property or potential danger to other horses or people.

10. Right of Livestock Lien.

Language here details the right of exerting a livestock lien and under what circumstances.

Also, very important to note clearly that this agreement will constitute a BILL OF SALE in the event of a lien.

Also should have separate initial line for Owner to acknowledge that he/she has read and understands the right of lien.

11. Release of Horse to Third Party.

Important to note here that Stable will not release the horse to a "third party" without written authorization by Owner.

THE FOLLOWING PORTION OF AGREEMENT INCLUDES SUGGESTED LEGAL LANGUAGE THAT SHOULD NOT BE CHANGED. STRONGLY ADVISE LANGUAGE DETAILING ALTERNATIVE DISPUTE RESOLUTION.

12. Assumption of Risk, Hold Harmless and Indemnification.

(a) Assumption of Risk. Owner acknowledges that he/she voluntarily participates in various equestrian activities on the premises of Stable and accepts the risks inherent with those activities.

(b) Hold Harmless. Owner understands that there are inherent risks associated with equine activities to Owner, Stable, persons and animals upon the premises and to property incidental to boarding horses at Stable. Owner has received, read, and signed a "Participant Agreement." Therefore, it is agreed, as one of the material considerations and inducements for the Stable boarding the horse, the Owner hereby releases, waives, discharges, covenants not to sue and assumes all risk of loss or damage, of whatsoever kind, nature or description, to Owner or Owner's property or to the person or property of another, as a result of, or arising out of the boarding of the horse at the Stable.

Owner further agrees to release and hold Stable harmless from all loss occasioned by fire, theft, vandalism, lightning, floods and/or other acts of God.

(c) Indemnification. Further, the Owner agrees to indemnify and hold Stable harmless from all damages, actions, causes of actions, claims, attorney's fees, costs, liabilities and losses that the Stable might incur as a consequence of having boarded the Owner's horse.

Owner hereby acknowledges and agrees to indemnify and hold harmless Stable and Stable's employees, representatives, and agents

Owner's initials: _____

13. Changes, Default, Termination, and Notice.

(a) Changes. Any modifications or additions must be in writing and signed by both parties to this agreement. No oral modifications or additions will be considered to be part of this agreement unless reduced to writing and signed by both parties.

(b) Default. Either party may terminate this agreement for failure of the other party to meet any material terms of this agreement. In the case of any default or breach by one party, the other party shall have the right to recover attorney's fees and court costs as a result of said default.

(c) Termination.

(i) Owner. Owner agrees that thirty (30) days notice shall be given to Stable as to the termination of this agreement. Early termination of this agreement does not relieve Owner of fees due for the remaining term of agreement unless otherwise agreed by Stable, or for any fees past due and owing.

(ii) Stable. Stable reserves the right of immediate termination for (a) failure of Owner to pay in full all fees and charges within a thirty-day billing cycle, (b) if said horse develops undesirable behaviors that are not conducive to Stable operations or it becomes dangerous to either life or property, or (c) for good cause, including but not limited to, Stable's belief that Owner has contributed to or created disruption or disharmony of the Stable operations. Stable agrees to give Owner thirty (30) days notice of termination of this agreement for any reasons other than those identified as cause for immediate termination.

(d) Notice. Any notice under this agreement shall be addressed in writing to the parties by certified mail or other means of verifiable notice to the recipient at its address set forth below. Parties are responsible for notification of any change of contact information and such changes shall be in writing.

14. Limitation of Actions and Resolution of Disputes.

(a) Limitation of Action. Any action or claim brought for breach of this agreement or for loss or claims due to negligence (ordinary and gross) must be brought within one (1) year of the date such claim or loss occurs.

(b) Alternative Dispute Resolution. The Stable and Owner mutually agree that, prior to formal litigation, any and all disputes arising in connection with this agreement or claims of loss due to negligence (active or passive) shall be addressed either through mediation or collaboration resolution methods. Excluded from alternative dispute resolution methods shall be the Stable's right of livestock lien in compliance with §16-401 of the Commercial Law Annotated Code of Maryland.

(i) Mediation. Disputes arising in connection with this agreement or claims of loss due to negligence may be addressed in one or more mediation sessions conducted by a certified Mediator. The Stable shall select a mediator familiar with equines and equine activities from a list presented to and acceptable to the Owner. Such mediation shall take place in a location reasonably convenient to both parties. The party initiating such mediation shall bear the costs of mediation.

(ii) Collaborative. Disputes arising in connection with this agreement or claims of loss due to negligence not addressed through mediation shall be addressed through the collaborative process. Both parties shall retain an attorney that has been collaboratively trained and agree to enter into the process in good faith and with full participation of the process (including, but not limited to, the use of the collaborative team approach). Parties shall bear the costs of retaining their own collaboratively trained attorneys and such other fees associated with the collaborative process.

(c) Litigation. In the event a dispute between Stable and Owner is not resolved by mediation or through the collaborative process and litigation ensues, the prevailing party shall be entitled to all costs associated with bringing suit or defending against a suit, including but not limited to, court costs and reasonable attorney fees.

15. Assignment. This agreement cannot be assigned by the Owner without the express written consent of Stable.

16. Applicable Law and Venue. The parties agree that the laws and jurisdiction of the State of Maryland govern this agreement. Venue for jurisdictional purposes shall be in _____ County.

17. Entire Agreement. This agreement constitutes the sole and entire agreement between the Stable and Owner and supersedes all prior agreements, negotiations, and discussions between the parties, with respect to the subject matter of this agreement.

18. Severability. Should any provision of this agreement be held invalid or illegal, such invalidity or illegality shall not invalidate the whole of this agreement; rather the agreement shall be construed as if it did not contain the invalid or illegal part, and the rights and obligations of the parties shall be construed and enforced accordingly.

EXECUTED on this_____ day of_____, 20_____.

STABLE:

OWNER (or Authorized Agent):

_____
Signature

_____
Signature

_____
Print Name

_____
Print Name

_____
Street Address

_____
Street Address

_____
City, State, Zip Code

_____
City, State, Zip Code

_____
Email Address

_____
Email Address

_____
Telephone – office

_____
Telephone – home

_____
Telephone – cellular

_____
Telephone – cellular

_____
Electronic mail address

_____
Alternate telephone

_____
Electronic mail address

**Lease Agreements may be for
Free Lease, Parital Lease, Limited Use,
Full Lease, or Lease with Option to Purchase**

STABLE NAME
Address
City, State, Zip Code
LEASE AGREEMENT

This Lease is made this_____day of _____, 20___ between STABLE NAME (hereinafter referred to as "Lessor"), and (name)_____residing at (address) (hereinafter referred to as "Lessee").

1. Term. [Specify here what the term of the lease is for and if there are options such as option to purchase or if it is a limited use lease.] The term of this Lease shall be for a period of_____ , beginning on (date)_____ and ending no later than (date)_____,or as otherwise provided for herein.

   [If lease with Option to Purchase will need purchase price of horse and deadline for when option is no longer available.]

2. Description of Horse. This Lease covers the horse as described in this section below (be as descriptive as possible):

3. Ownership of Horse. Lessor warrants that Lessor has good and clear title to said horse free from any liens and has the right to execute this Lease.

4. Consideration/Payments. In consideration of $_____ per horse per month paid by Lessee in advance of the first day of each month, Stable agrees to lease the above described horse.

5. Warranties of Lessee. (May include language of Lessee's riding skills.)

6. Exercise and Care. (Language that horse will be used at the training level or ability of horse and rider's skills. Language that Lessee agrees to take all reasonable actions to maintain said horse in good health and to minimize risk to the health and safety of Lessee and horse.)

7. Uses of Horse and Limitations. Lessee covenants to use the horse for Lessee's sole benefit and not to use the horse for any purpose other than set forth: _____

8. Hold Harmless.(Language indemnifying Stable or Owner from third-party liability; Lessee accepting risks.)

9. Default. (Standard default language.)

.10. Resolution of Disputes. (Language detailing method(s) of resolving disputes.)

11. Governing Law. This Agreement shall be construed in accordance with and shall be governed by the laws of the State of Maryland.

12. Entire Agreement. This constitutes the entire Agreement between the parties. Any modifications or additions must be in writing and signed by both parties to this Agreement. No oral modifications or additions will be considered to be part of this Agreement unless reduced to writing and signed by both parties.

SIGNED this_____ day of _____, 20___.

LESSOR:

LESSEE:

_____

_____

Signature
Stable Name/ Horse Owner

Signature

STABLE NAME
Stable or Livestock Dealer License
Address
City, State, Zip Code

Equine Purchase and Sale Agreement (Cash Contract)

THIS AGREEMENT is made by and between_____
("Buyer") and _____("Seller") for purchase and sale of an equine ("equine" shall mean any pony, horse, mule, or donkey). Buyer desires to purchase from Seller and Seller desires to sell to Buyer the equine described herein. The parties agree to be legally bound by the terms and conditions of this agreement.

Description
Equine's Name:_____
By:_____Out of:_____
Breed:_____ ❑ filly   ❑ mare   ❑ colt   ❑ stallion   ❑ gelding
Foaled:_____or approx. age_____ or ❑ age unknown   Size: _____
Color & Markings: _____
Registration # or Tattoo (if applicable):_____

A. CONSIDERATION. In consideration of the total sum of _____
U.S. Dollars ($_____), Seller agrees to sell Buyer the equine described above and Buyer agrees to buy said equine on the terms set forth herein.

B. PAYMENT TERMS.
(1) This purchase is for cash and Buyer agrees to pay _____
U.S. Dollars ($_____) as deposit on the (date)_____and   the balance due of_____U.S. Dollars ($_____) payable on (date) _____.

(2) In the event sales or use taxes are assessed by any governmental authority as a result of the sale and purchase hereby made, Buyer shall pay to Seller, in addition to the purchase price, such amount of such sales or use taxes as may be so assessed.

C. DELIVERY. Delivery of the horse shall be construed to mean the time at which the equine is loaded on a trailer and removed from Seller's facilities (or other moment in time mutually agreed). Buyer is responsible for all costs, risks and liabilities associated with transportation of the equine.

D. PRE-PURCHASE VETERINARIAN EXAMINATION.
(1) Seller encourages Buyer to have a pre-purchase examination conducted by a qualified and licensed veterinarian of Buyer's choice. Buyer is responsible for all costs association with said examination. The examination shall take place at Seller's facility at a mutually agreeable date and time. Buyer or Buyer's agent may attend the examination. Upon completion of the veterinarian examination and a favorable acceptance of the report by Buyer, Buyer agrees to purchase said horse **"as is"** and **"with all faults."**

(2) If the equine does not satisfactorily pass the pre-purchase veterinarian examination, the Buyer has the option to decline the purchase of the equine and void this Agreement. Any payments made to Seller in anticipation of a final sale shall be returned to Buyer.

E. BUYER'S ACKNOWLEDGES. Buyer acknowledges that an opportunity to inspect the equine, including the use of a qualified, licensed veterinarian, has been offered and conducted and Buyer is satisfied with the equine's condition, or in lieu of a veterinarian examination, that Buyer has voluntarily declined the offer for inspection by a qualified, licensed veterinarian and has opted to visually inspect the equine personally or by an agent and is satisfied with the equine's condition.

F. WARRANTIES.

(1) Seller warrants _____ is an authorized agent of Seller for the purpose of completing the transaction for the sale of said equine.

(2) Seller warrants that Seller/Agent is a consigner and licensed to sell horse livestock in the State of Maryland. The owner of said equine has authorized Seller to act as his/her agent in the transaction for the sale of the said equine.

(3) Seller warrants the above equine to be free and clear of all encumbrances.

(4) Seller warrants the name, sire, dam, gender, foaling date and registration number as set forth in this agreement.

(5) Seller makes no other warranties or representations, express or implied, with respect to the equine, including warranties concerning the physical condition, health or soundness of the horse and warranties of merchantability or fitness for any particular purpose. Parties acknowledge that the equine is sold "as is" and "with all faults."

(6) Should Buyer discover within X number of days (___) from date of delivery of equine and/or registration papers that any of the above warranties have failed, Seller agrees to cure the deficiency to the best of Buyer's ability in a timely fashion.

G. REGISTRATION AND OWNERSHIP TRANSFERS. Upon payment in full, Seller agrees to execute all necessary papers and to take all steps necessary to transfer ownership and registration of the equine to Buyer within a reasonable number of dys – typically two weeks (_____) days from Buyer's check or certified funds being accepted and cleared by Seller's bank.

H. RISK OF LOSS. Pending delivery to Buyer, Seller shall assume the risk of loss of said equine. Upon delivery, Buyer shall assume the risks of loss. Delivery shall be construed to be the time at which the equine is loaded on a trailer and removed from Seller's or Seller's agent's facilities.

I. DEFAULT. This Agreement is terminated upon a breach of any material term and the non-breaching party has the right to collect all reasonable fees and costs, including attorney fees, incurred due to the breach from the breaching party.

J. LIMITATION OF ACTIONS and RESOLUTION OF DISPUTES.

(1) Limitation of Action. Any action or claim brought by either party for breach of this agreement or for loss due to negligence (active or passive) must be brought within one (1) year of the date such claim or loss occurs. The parties agree to this time limit and further waive any rights available under any State statute of limitations.

(2) **Mediation (Collaboration language may also be added to this** section). The parties mutually agree that, prior to formal litigation, any and all disputes arising in connection with this Agreement or claims of loss due to negligence (active or passive) shall be addressed in one or more mediation sessions conducted by a certified Mediator familiar with equine and equine activities. The breaching party shall select the Mediator from a list acceptable to the non-breaching party. Such mediation shall take place in a mutually agreeable location convenient to both parties within the jurisdictional county noted in "Governing Law" of this agreement. The cost for securing mediation services shall be shared equally by both parties.

(3) Litigation. In the event mediation fails and litigation is thereafter initiated by either party, the prevailing party shall be entitled to all reasonable costs incurred together with reasonable attorney's fees, including any attorney fees incurred incidental to a successful appeal.

K. GOVERNING LAW. This Agreement shall be construed in accordance with and shall be governed by the laws of the State of Maryland. The parties agree that any legal action shall be brought in _____ _____County, Maryland.

L. SEVERABILITY. If any portion of this Agreement is held invalid, it is agreed that the balance shall, notwithstanding, continue in full force and effect.

M. ENTIRE AGREEMENT. This constitutes the entire Agreement between the parties. Any modifications or additions must be in writing and signed by both parties to this Agreement. No oral modifications, additions, prior agreements or understandings will be considered to be part of this Agreement unless reduced to writing and signed by both parties.

This contract may be signed in two parts, but shall be construed as one whole contract, and valid from the latest date of the two. Facsimile signatures shall be accepted as an original signature.

EXECUTED this____day of_____, 20_____, at _____, Maryland by Seller.

EXECUTED this____day of_____, 20_____, at _____,by Buyer

SELLER: BUYER:

_____   _____
Signature   Signature

_____   _____
Printed Name   Printed Name

_____   _____
Street Address   Street Address

_____   _____
City, State, Zip Code   City, State, Zip Code

Stable Name
Stable License #
Address
City, State, Zip Code

Purchase and Sale Agreement
(Installment)

THIS AGREEMENT is made between_____("Buyer") and _____
_____ ("Seller") for purchase and sale of the equine ("equine" shall mean any pony, horse, mule, or donkey) described below on the following terms and conditions of sale:

Name:_____
Breed: _____
Age (D.O.B.):_____Gender: _____
Color and Markings: _____
Registration No: _____
Tattoo (if applicable)_____

A. CONSIDERATION
In consideration of the total sum of_____U.S. Dollars ($_____
_____), Seller agrees to sell Buyer the equine described herein and Buyer agrees to buy said equine on the terms set forth herein.

B. PAYMENT TERMS
(1) A down payment of $_____ due (date)_____. The balance of $ _____ shall be paid by Buyer over (_____) months.
The first payment shall be due on (date)_____ and payments in the amount of
$_____shall be due and owing on or prior to the_____ day of each month thereafter. A final payment in the amount of $_____
shall be paid on (date)_____.
 (2) Payments may be made by personal check, cashier's check or money order made payable to Seller.
(3) A $_____ fee for returned checks shall be paid by Buyer and Buyer shall be obligated to provide future payments by certified funds only.
(4) Any amount due and owing more than __x number of_____days overdue shall bear interest at the rate of___percentage (_____%) per month from the billing date, which is equivalent to_____
_____percent (%) per annum. If for any reason attempts to collect sums owed are initiated, Buyer will be required to pay all attorney's fees and costs related to collections.
(5) In the event sales or use taxes are assessed by any governmental authority as a result of the sale and purchase hereby made, Buyer shall pay to Seller, in addition to the purchase price, such amount of such sales or use taxes as may be so assessed.
(6) Should Buyer fail to make said payment, Seller shall have the option to declare the balance of the Note then owing to be due and payable.

C. SECURITY INTEREST and INSURANCE
(1) Security Interest. Seller shall retain a security interest in the equine until payment is received in full. Buyer shall not register said equine as the owner until payment is received in full by Seller. Further, Buyer shall not sell the equine until payment is received in full without prior written consent by Seller.

(2) Insurance. Pending full payment for purchase of said equine, Buyer agrees to indemnify and hold Seller harmless from any injury to any person(s) or animal(s) or damage to any property caused by said equine, and shall carry liability insurance to covers such liability with $_____personal injury and $_____ for damage to property and $_____ per accident and to name Seller as additional insured.

D. DELIVERY. Delivery of the equine shall be construed to mean the time at which the equine is loaded on a trailer and removed from Seller's facilities (or other agreed moment in time should be written in this paragraph). Buyer is responsible for all costs and risks and liabilities associated with transportation of the equine.

E. PRE-PURCHASE VETERINARIAN EXAMINATION.

(1) Seller encourages Buyer to have a pre-purchase examination conducted by a qualified and licensed veterinarian of Buyer's choice. Buyer is responsible for all costs association with said examination. The examination shall take place at Seller's facility at a mutually agreeable date and time. Buyer or Buyer's agent may attend the examination. Upon completion of the veterinarian examination and a favorable acceptance of the report by Buyer, Buyer agrees to purchase said equine **"as is."**

(2) If the equine does not satisfactorily pass the pre-purchase veterinarian examination, the Buyer has the option to decline the purchase of the equine and void this Agreement.

F. WARRANTIES.

(1) Seller warrants _____ is an authorized agent of Seller for the purpose of completing the transaction for the sale of said equine.

(2) Seller warrants that Seller/Agent is a consigner and licensed to sell equine livestock in the State of Maryland. The owner of said equine has authorized Seller to act as his/her agent in the transaction for the sale of the said equine.

(3) Seller warrants the above equine to be free and clear of all encumbrances.

(4) Seller warrants the name, sire, dam, gender, foaling date and registration number as set forth in this agreement.

(5) Seller makes no other warranties or representations, express or implied, with respect to the equine, including warranties concerning the physical condition, health or soundness of the equine and warranties of merchantability or fitness for any particular purpose. Parties acknowledge that the equine is sold **"as is"** and **"with all faults."**

(6) Should Buyer discover within x number of days (___) from date of delivery of equine and/or registration papers that any of the above warranties have failed, Seller agrees to cure the deficiency to the best of their ability in a timely fashion.

G. BUYER'S ACKNOWLEDGES. Buyer acknowledges that either an opportunity to inspect the equine, including the use of a qualified, licensed veterinarian, has been offered and conducted and Buyer is satisfied with the equine's condition, or that Buyer has voluntarily declined the offer for inspection by a qualified, licensed veterinarian and has opted to visually inspect the equine personally or by an agent and is satisfied with the equine's condition. If Buyer has rejected the pre-purchase examination by a qualified veterinarian, Buyer accepts the equine as **"as-is"** and **"with all faults"** and any and all warranties herein made are waived.

H. REGISTRATION AND OWNERSHIP TRANSFERS. Upon payment in full, Seller agrees to execute all necessary papers and to take all steps necessary to transfer ownership and registration of the equine to Buyer, at no cost to Buyer, within fourteen (14) days from Buyer's check or certified funds being accepted and cleared by Seller's bank.

I. RISK OF LOSS. Pending delivery to Buyer, Seller shall assume the risk of loss of said equine. Upon delivery, Buyer shall assume the risks of loss. Delivery shall be construed to be the time at which the equine is loaded on a trailer and removed from Seller's or Seller's agent's facilities.

J. DEFAULT.

(1) Upon material breach of this Agreement, Seller reserves the right to remove said equine without incurring any responsibility to Lessee.

(2) This Agreement is terminated upon a breach of any material term and the other party has the right to collect all reasonable fees and costs, including attorney fees, from the breaching party.

K. LIMITATION OF ACTIONS and RESOLUTION OF DISPUTES.

(1) Limitation of Action. Any action or claim brought by either party for breach of this agreement or for loss due to negligence (active or passive) must be brought within one (1) year of the date such claim or loss occurs.

(2) Mediation (Collaboration language may also be added if client agrees.). The parties mutually agree that, prior to formal litigation, any and all disputes arising in connection with this Agreement or claims of loss due to negligence (active or passive) shall be addressed in one or more mediation sessions conducted by a certified Mediator. The breaching-party shall select the Mediator familiar with equine and

equine activities from a list acceptable to the non-breaching party. Such mediation shall take place in a mutually agreeable location convenient to both parties. The cost for securing mediation services shall be shared equally by both parties.

(3) Litigation. In the event mediation fails and litigation is initiated by either party, the prevailing party shall be entitled to all reasonable costs incurred together with reasonable attorney's fees, including any attorney fees incurred incidental to a successful appeal.

L. GOVERNING LAW. This Agreement shall be construed in accordance with and shall be governed by the laws of the State of Maryland. Any legal action must be brought in_____ County, Maryland.

M. ENTIRE AGREEMENT. This constitutes the entire Agreement between the parties. Any modifications or additions must be in writing and signed by both parties to this Agreement. No oral modifications or additions will be considered to be part of this Agreement unless reduced to writing and signed by both parties. If any portion of this Agreement is held invalid, it is agreed that the balance shall, notwithstanding, continue in full force and effect.

This contract may be signed in two parts, but shall be construed as one whole contract, and valid from the latest date of the two. Facsimile signatures shall be accepted as an original signature.

EXECUTED this_____day of _____, 20_____, at _____, Maryland by Seller/Agent.

EXECUTED this_____day of _____, 20_____, at _____, by Buyer.

SELLER: BUYER:

_____   _____
Signature   Signature

_____   _____
Printed Name   Printed Name

_____   _____
Street Address   Street Address

_____   _____
City, State, Zip Code   City, State, Zip Code

Promissory Note

_____   _____
Total Amount of Note   Date of Note

     FOR VALUE RECEIVED, <u>(Debtor/Buyer)</u>_____
promises to pay to the order of (Seller of Horse)_____
_____, (Price of Horse)_____
$_____) Dollars, without offset, in one lump sum payment due on or before (<u>date pay-</u>
<u>ment due)</u>_____.

     Payment shall be payable at the address of <u>(Name of Seller)</u>_____
located at <u>(Address of Seller)</u>_____
and payable on <u>(date payment due)</u>_____. Said payment is due
default thereof, said monies owed shall at the option of the holder and without further notice become
immediately due and payable. If, as a result of said default, this note is placed in the hands of an attorney for collection, I hereby agree to pay a reasonable attorney's fee of twenty (20%) percent of the
amount due and owing of this defaulted note.

     To secure payment of this note, I hereby authorize, irrevocably, the Clerk of Court or any Attorney
of any Court of Record to appear for me in such Court, at any time before or after maturity of said note
and confess a judgment against me in favor of any holder of this Note with or without filing an Aver-
ment of Default, with release of errors, without stay of execution, and for such amount as may appear to
be paid thereon, together with charges, attorney's fees and costs as herein provided, and I hereby waive
and release all benefit and relief from any and all appraisement, stay or exemption under the laws of any
State, now in force or hereafter to be passed.

WITNESS:_____   DEBTOR:_____

Equine Bill of Sale

Date _____

For and in consideration of _____ Dollars ($_____
____) paid in full and receipt of which is hereby acknowledged I, _____, hereby
sell, assign, transfer and set over unto_____my entire right, title
and interest in and to the equine as described below:

Equine's Name:_____
By:_____Out of:_____
Breed:_____
Foaled:_____Gender:_____Size:_____
Color & Markings: _____
Registration # or Tattoo (if applicable):_____

(1) Seller warrants the description as set forth above is true and accurate to the best of Seller's knowledge.

(2) Seller warrants the above horse to be free and clear of all encumbrances and Seller has the legal authority to transfer ownership to Buyer.

(3) Seller makes no other warranties or representations, express or implied, with respect to the equine, including warranties concerning the physical condition, health or soundness of the horse and warranties of merchantability or fitness for any particular purpose.

(4) Buyer and Seller acknowledge a "Sale and Purchase Agreement" for the above horse has been executed and all terms and conditions have been met.

(5) Buyer acknowledges an opportunity to inspect the equine, including the use of a qualified veterinarian, has been offered and/or conducted and is satisfied with the equine's condition.

(6) Parties acknowledge that the equine is sold "as is" and "with all faults."

_____   _____
Signature of Witness for Seller   Signature of Seller

_____   _____
Print Name of Witness for Seller   Print Name of Seller

_____   _____
Signature of Witness of Buyer   Signature of Buyer

_____   _____
Print Name of Witness for Buyer   Print Name of Buyer

_____

If no witnesses, a notary public shall witness the execution of this Bill of Sale.

STATE OF MARYLAND; COUNTY OF _____
Subscribed and sworn to me before me on this _____ day of_____, 20____.

My commission expires _____.

_____
Notary Public Signature

Seal

Maryland Statutory Lien on Livestock

MD Code, Commercial Law

Title 16. Statutory Liens on Personal Property

Subtitle 4 – Lien on Livestock

§ 16-401. Care or Custody

(a) The owner or operator of a livery stable or other establishment who gives care or custody to any livestock has a lien on the livestock for any reasonable charge incurred for:

    (1) Board and custody;

    (2) Training;

    (3) Veterinarians' and blacksmiths' services; and

    (4) Other proper maintenance expenses.

(b) If the charges which give rise to the lien are due and unpaid for 30 days and the lienor is in possession of the livestock, the lienor may sell the livestock to which the lien attaches at public sale.

(c) (1) The lienor shall publish notice of the sale once a week for two successive weeks in one or more newspapers of general circulation in the county where the livestock is located.

(2) In addition, the lienor shall send notice by registered or certified mail at least 30 days before the sale to the owner of the livestock at his last known address. If the owner's address is unknown, the notice may be given by posting it on the door of the courthouse or on a bulletin board in the immediate vicinity of the door of the courthouse of the county where the livestock is located.

(d) (1) The proceeds of the sale shall be applied, in the following order, to:

    (i) the expenses of the sale; and

    (ii) the amount of the lien claim.

(2) After application of the proceeds in accordance with paragraph (1) of this subsection, any remaining balance shall be paid to the owner of the livestock.

Lien Release
[Stable Name]
[Address]

Pursuant to Maryland Commercial Law § 16-401 (Livestock Lien), [STABLE] had placed a lien on the horse described below. For and in consideration of payment for arrearages and related expenses in the amount of _____Dollars ($_____), receipt of which is hereby acknowledged, as an Agent for and on behalf of [STABLE], the lien interest held by [STABLE] in and to the equine as described below is hereby released to _____
_____ ("Payee"):

    Horse's Name:_____

    By: _____Out of:_____

    Breed:_____

    Foaled:_____Gender: _____Size: _____

    Color & Markings: _____

    Registration # or Tattoo (if applicable):_____

WITNESSED HERETO:

[Stable]

_____   _____
Signature of Agent   Date

_____   _____
Signature of Payee   Date

_____
Printed Name of Payee

_____
Address

_____
State, City, Zip Code

State Board of Veterinary Medical Examiners
Complaint Form

1. YOUR INFORMATION:

Name: _____   Pet's name: _____ Age: _____

Area code and telephone: _____   Species: _____ Breed: _____

Address: _____   Date(s) of treatment: _____
          Street Address   Reason(s) for visit: _____

_____   _____
       City, State, Zip code   _____

2. COMPLAINT AGAINST:

Veterinarian's Name: _____   Clinic's name: _____

Clinic's address: _____

3. IF OTHER VETERINARIANS TREATED YOUR PET AFTER THE VETERINARIAN LISTED ABOVE, PLEASE PROVIDE THEIR INFORMATION BELOW:

Veterinarian's Name: _____   Clinic's name: _____

Clinic's address: _____

Veterinarian's Name: _____   Clinic's name: _____

Clinic's address: _____

4. HAVE YOU CONTACTED THE VETERINARIAN IN YOUR COMPLAINT?

Yes _____   No _____

If yes, what was the result? _____

_____

5. HAVE YOU RECEIVED ANY REIMBURSEMENT FROM THE VETERINARIAN OR VETERINARY HOSPITAL LISTED IN #2, ABOVE, FOR ANY EXPENSES YOU INCURRED AS A RESULT OF SERVICES PROVIDED YOUR PET?

Yes _____   No _____

6. IF THIS MATTER GOES TO A HEARING, WOULD YOU BE WILLING TO TESTIFY?

Yes _____   No _____

7. PROVIDE THE NAMES, ADDRESSES, AND TELEPHONE NUMBERS OF WITNESSES.

Name: _____   Name: _____

Address: _____   Address: _____
       Street Address   Street Address

_____   _____
     City, State, Zip Code   City, State, Zip Code

Area Code and Telephone: _____   Area Code and Telephone: _____

Maryland Department of Agriculture Necropsy Fees

Necropsy and carcass disposal fees are now separate (two separate fees will be charged).

Animal	Necropsy in state	Necropsy out of state	Disposal
Dogs and Cats			
<80 lbs	$250	$300	$40 ($50 out state)
>80 lbs	$275	$350	$0.50 / lb in state $0.75 /lb out of state
Food Animal*			
<300 lbs	$125	$150	No charge**in state $0.75/lb out of state
>300 lbs	$175	$225	No charge**in state $0.75/lb out of state
Equine			
Horse > 300 lbs	$275	$375	$0.50 / lb in state $0.75 /lb out of state
Fetus, foal ≤ 300 lb	$125	$150	No charge
With spinal cord examination	$500	$600	$0.50 / lb in state $0.75 /lb out of state
Insurance case	$375	$525	$0.50 / lb in state $0.75 /lb out of state
Poultry	No charge	No charge	No charge **
Ratites, camelids			
<250 lb	$125	$150	$40 ($50 out state)
>250 lb	$275	$375	$0.50/ lb in state $0.75 /lb out of state
Exotics, managed species*	$200	$250	$0.50 / lb in state $0.75 /lb out of state

* Food animals are cattle, sheep, goats, swine
** Necropsy and disposal are subsidized by federal disease control funds
*** Exotics include "pocket pets", reptiles and amphibians. Managed species are
animals kept in zoological parks, mink, and free living wild animals (rabbits, fox, raccoon, etc)

DISPOSAL/CREMATION FEES:

	In State	Out of State
Disposal only, any species		
< 80 lbs	$40	$50
> 80 lbs	$0.50/ lb	$0.75 / lb
Incineration, multiple animals (commercial)*	$0.75 lb	$0.90 / lb
In-county government	$0.50 / lb	NA
Rendering after necropsy**	$350	$450
Specific Ash Return		
Small animal (<80 lbs)	Disposal + $70	Disposal + $150
Small animal (>80 lbs)	Disposal + $70	Disposal + $150
Large animal ***	Disposal + $300	Disposal + $ 400
Generic Ash Return		
Small animal (<80 lb)	Disposal + $50	Disposal + $100
Small animal (>80 lb)	Disposal + $50	Disposal + $100
Large animal ***	Disposal + $100	Disposal + $200

* commercial = animal control, local veterinarians, commercial entities
** Rendering after necropsy: instead of disposal by cremation at $0.50 per pound,
flat rate of $350 in state or $450 out of state; applies only to horses
*** Large animals are cattle, pigs, goats, sheep, horses, camelids, exotics

Appendices

Maryland Animal Control by County
Contact information and regulation sampling

Allegany County
Animal Control: http://gov.allconet.org/animal/laws.htm
Location: 716 Furnace Street, Cumberland, Maryland 21502
Telephone: 301-777-5930
Animal Control Laws: Chapter 117, Section 16 – Dogs Attacking Other Animals or Humans

> Any person may kill any dog which he sees in the act of pursing, attacking, wounding or killing any human being, or any poultry or livestock, whether or not such dog bears the proper license tag required by this chapter. There shall be no liability upon such person or persons in damages or otherwise for such killing. All such cases shall be promptly reported to the ASP and be investigated by ASP.

Anne Arundel County
Animal Control: http://www.aacounty.org/AnimalControl/index.cfm
Location: 411 Maxwell Frye Road, Millersville, Maryland 21108
Telephone: (410) 222-8900
E-mail: P98871@aacounty.org
Animal Control Laws: numerous County Code sections relevant to use of horses

Baltimore City
Bureau of Animal Control: http://www.baltimorehealth.org/animalcontrol.html#regulations
Location: 301 Stockholm Street, Baltimore, Maryland 21230
Telephone: 410-396-4698
Animal Control Laws: "Exotic Animal Regulations – Horses"

> On August 6, 2007, the Baltimore City Health Department (Department) promulgated Regulations regarding the keeping of certain exotic pets and other animals. See Wild and Exotic Animals: Prohibited. The following provides additional commentary and guidance on the keeping of horses as allowed under the new Regulations. The Regulations provide 6 methods for horses to

be in Baltimore. These methods are:

1. Horses that are actively engaged for use in a licensed Arabber and/or carriage trade.
2. Horses used in a zoological park.
3. Horses used as part of a research facility licensed under the Federal Animal Welfare Act.
4. Horses in a circus or owned by a native wildlife rehabilitator licensed by federal, state, or City permit.
5. Horses working for a law enforcement agency.
6. Horses used under Section 2 (d) of the regulations where the Bureau of Animal Control has "permitted and approved" a "venue to exhibit or use animals which has adequate operating protective measures to prevent these animals from becoming a public nuisance, injuring the public, or causing a public health threat."

In order to justify a permit under (6), the owner shall show the following:

a. Sheltering of the horses is in an approved stable. The stable must be licensed in accordance with state and local law. The stable and stall space must be capable of providing adequate space based on current nationally recognized humane standards and as mandated by state and local laws.
b. Because these horses shall be considered pleasure horses, the facilities and proposed exercise space must meet nationally recognized humane standards, as set forth by nationally recognized humane organizations that provide guidelines for proper and adequate exercise space for such horses.
c. Evidence of a Certificate of Equine Liability Insurance in the amount of $50,000.
d. Department approval of a plan detailing the intended "exhibition" or "use" of the animals.

The Department may convene an independent panel of equine humane experts to review the permit application.

Baltimore County

Animal Control: http://www.baltimorecountymd.gov/Agencies/health/diseasecontrol/animalcontrol/index.html
Location: 13800 Manor Road, Baldwin, Maryland 21012
Telephone: 410-887-5961
E-mail: animalcontrol@baltimorecountymd.gov
Animal Control Laws: Article 12: Animals §§ 12-1-101 et seq.

Calvert County

Location: Tri-County Animal Shelter (serving Calvert, Charles and St. Mary's counties)
6707 Animal Shelter Road, Hughesville, Maryland 20637
Telephone: 410-535-1600 x 304
Animal Control Regulations: http://www.co.cal.md.us/assets/ordinance.pdf

Caroline County
Caroline County Humane Society
Location: 407 West Bell Street, Ridgely, MD 21660
Telephone: 410-820-1600
Animal Control Regulations: http://www.ecode360.com/?custId=CA1090

Carroll County
Humane Society of Carroll County
Location: 2517 Littlestown Pike, Westminster, Maryland 21157
Telephone: 410-848-4810
E-mail: cratliff@ccg.carr.org
Animal Control Regulations: http://ccgovernment.carr.org/ccg/code/
index.asp

Cecil County
Cecil County SPCA, Inc.
Location: 3280 Augustine Herman Highway, Chesapeake City, Maryland
21915
Telephone: 410-398-9555 or 410-885-2342
Animal Control Regulations/County Code: http://www.ecode360.
com/?custId=CE0748

Charles County
Location: Tri-County Animal Shelter (serving Calvert, Charles and St.
Mary's counties)
6707 Animal Shelter Road, Hughesville, Maryland 20637
Telephone: 301-609-3425
Animal Control Regulations: http://www.charlescounty.org/es/
animalcontrol/regulations.pdf

Dorchester County
Humane Society of Dorchester County
Location: 4930 Bucktown Road, Cambridge, Maryland 21613
Telephone: (410) 228-3083 or 410-228-3090
Animal Control Regulations: http://ecode360.com/?custid=do0950

Frederick County
Frederick County Animal Control
Location: 1832 Rosemont Avenue, Frederick, Maryland 21702
Telephone: 301-600-1546 or Animal Control Officers: 301-600-1544
Code:http://www.amlegal.com/nxt/gateway.dll/Maryland/frederickco_md/frederickcou
ntymarylandcodeofordinances?f=templates$fn=default.htm$3.0$vid=amlegal:frederickco_
md

Garrett County

Garrett County Animal Shelter and Animal Control
Location: 152 Oakland Sang Run Road, Oakland, Maryland 21550
Telephone: 301-334-3553

Harford County

Animal Control
Location: 611 North Fountain Green Road, Bel Air, Maryland 21014
Telephone: 410-638-3505
Animal Control Regulations: http://www.harfordcountymd.gov/dilp/animal_control.html

Howard County

Animal Control Operations
Location: 8576 Davis Road, Columbia, Maryland 21045
Telephone: 410-313-2780
Animal Control Regulations: http://www.co.ho.md.us/servicesresidents_animals.htm#anch23330
> "Killed or Injured Livestock. (Howard County) Animal Control staff (410-313-2780), in cooperation with the Cooperative Extension Service, will investigate claims of killed or injured livestock. Forms are available for residents to complete immediately after such incidents."

Kent County

The Humane Society of Kent County, Maryland, Inc.
Location: 10720 Augustine Herman Highway, Chestertown, Maryland 21620
Telephone: 410-778-3648 or 1-866-661-7387
Website: www.kenthuman.org
County Code: http://www.e-codes.generalcode.com/codebook_frameset.asp?ep=fs&lg=1&t=ws&cb=1414_A

Montgomery County

Division of Animal Control and Humane Treatment
Telephone: 240-773-5960
CountyCode: http://www.amlegal.com/nxt/gateway.dll?f=templates &fn=default.htm&vid=amlegal:montgomeryco_md_mc

Prince George's County

Dept. of Environmental Resources, Animal Management Division
Location: 8311 D'Arcy Road, Forestville, Maryland 20747
Telephone: 301-499-8300
County Code: http://egov.co.pg.md.us/lis/

Queen Anne's County

Queen Anne's County Department of Animal Services
Locaton: 201 Clay Drive, Queenstown, Maryland 21658
Telephone: 410-758-3493
County Code: http://www.ecode360.com/?custId=QU1770

St. Mary's County

Location: Tri-County Animal Shelter (serving Calvert, Charles and St. Mary's counties)
6707 Animal Shelter Road, Hughesville, Maryland 20637
Telephone: 301-475-8018
Animal Control Regulations: http://www.charlescounty.org/es/animal control/regulations.pdf

Somerset County

Animal Control
Location: 7922 Crisfield Highway (Rte. 413), Westover, Maryland 21871
Telephone: 410-651-0986
Somerset County Extension Services: http://extension.umd.edu/local/ Somerset/

Talbot County

Animal Control / Talbot Human Society
Location: 7894 Ocean Gateway, PO Box 1143, Easton, Maryland 21601
Telephone: 410-822-0107
County Code: http://www.talbotcountymd.gov

Washington County

Humane Society of Washington County (privately contracted with County)
Location: 13011 Maugansville Road, Hagerstown, Maryland 21740
Telephone: 301-733-2060
County Code: http://www.washco-md.net/washco_2/pdf_files/legal/ CPLL2007.pdf

Wicomico County

Humane Society of Wicomico County (privately contracted with County)
Location: 5130 Citation Drive, Salisbury, Maryland 21804
Telephone: 410-749-7603
Website: www.wicomicohumane.org/
"For over 30 years, the Humane Society of Wicomico County has provided temporary shelter for the County's homeless and unwanted animals. Our services aren't just for dogs and cats…we've also helped horses, goats, rabbits and chickens." County Code: http://www.ecode360.com/?custId=WI0638

Worcester County

Location: Animal Control, 6201 Timmons Road, Snow Hill, Maryland 21863
Telephone: 410-632-1340
Animal Law Regulations/County Code: http://www.co.worcester.md.us/

APPENDIX TWO

Equine Insurance

Care, Custody and Control (CCC) Coverage

Typically covered: Risk of loss or injury to another person's horse in your care.

Not typically covered: Risk of loss or injury caused by horses in your care, loss or injury to your own horses.

Used by: Boarding stables, breeding farms, trainers and other commercial equine operations who take on the responsibility of caring for others' horses.

Commercial Equine Liability Coverage

Typically covered: General liability relating to operating your equine business.

Not typically covered: Risk of loss or injury to another person's horse in your care.

Used by: Boarding stables, breeding stables, trainers and sales barns.

Farm and Ranch Coverage

Typically covered: Loss to real and personal property.

Not typically covered: Loss of livestock, general liability.

Used by: Farm and ranch owners.

Workers' Compensation Coverage

Typically covered: Injuries to employees incurred as part of their job.

Not typically covered: Losses caused by your employees.

Used by: Employers.

Horse Trailer Insurance

Typically covered: Damage/loss to your trailer.

Not typically covered: damage/loss caused by your trailer.

Used by: Horse trailer owners.

Short-term Transit Coverage

Typically covered: Death during transit.

Not typically covered: Injuries during transit.

Used by: Horse owners hauling their horses on a short-term basis, who do not have mortality or major medical coverage.

Horse Owner Liability Coverage

Typically covered: Injuries or property damage caused by your horse.

Not typically covered: Business activities relating to your horse.

Used by: Horse owners concerned about being held liable for their horse's actions.

Equine Mortality and Theft Coverage

Typically covered: Theft and death not caused by the owner's negligence or willful misconduct.

Not typically covered: Death caused by owner's negligence or willful misconduct.

Used by: Owners of valuable horses.

Major Medical and Surgical Coverage

Typically covered: Certain types of surgery and other expensive medical procedures.

Not typically covered: Routine medical procedures.

Used by: Owners of valuable horses.

Loss of Use Coverage

Typically covered: Permanent disability of horse.

Not typically covered: Temporary disability, death.

Used by: Owners of valuable performance horses.

Named Perils Coverage

Typically covered: Death from certain causes (e.g. fire).

Not typically covered: Death from illness.

Used by: Horse owners who don't want (or cannot obtain) coverage under mortality or major medical coverage.

Show and Event Liability

<u>Typically covered:</u> Injuries, losses and property damage resulting from club activities.

<u>Not typically covered:</u> Contractual and other disputes relating to events.

<u>Used by:</u> Operators of horse shows, clinics and other events.

Riding Club and Other Group Coverage

<u>Typically covered:</u> Injuries, losses and property damage that occurs during club activities.

<u>Not typically covered:</u> Contractual and other disputes relating to club events.

<u>Used by:</u> 4-H Clubs, pony clubs and other horse-oriented clubs that host mounted events.

Race Horse Owner Liability Coverage

<u>Typically covered:</u> General liabilities associated with race horse ownership.

<u>Not typically covered:</u> Injury or loss of the horse, liability associated with activities that are more than mere ownership.

<u>Used by:</u> Race horse owners.

Stallion Infertility Coverage

<u>Typically covered:</u> Permanent loss of fertility/breeding ability.

<u>Not typically covered:</u> Death.

<u>Used by:</u> Breeding stallion owners.

Barren Mare Coverage

<u>Typically covered:</u> Permanent loss of fertility or breeding ability.

<u>Not typically covered:</u> Death.

<u>Used by:</u> Breeders.

APPENDIX THREE

Mediation
Case Summary (1992-2008)

Mediation Agreement Enforced

Reese v. Tingey Const., 177 P.3d 605, 2008 UT 7 (2008) (Personal Injury case: Utah laws protects confidentiality of mediation discussion and mediation agreement must be reduced to writing in order to be enforced by a court.)

Stewart v. Preston Pipeline, Inc., 36 Cal.Rptr.3d 901, 134 Cal. App.4th 1565 (2005) (Personal Injury case: California mediation confidentiality statue does not act as a shield to prevent admission of a purported settlement document signed at conclusion of mediation.)

Check v. Rosetti, 2003 WL 22251415, OhioApp 5 Dist., 2003 (Sept. 29, 2003) (Property dispute: intent of parties memorialized in mediation agreement is enforceable.)

Heller v. Pal, 2003 WL 22183957, Cal.App 1 Dist., 2003 (Sept. 23, 2003) (Partnership Agreement/Real Estate dispute: settlement agreement effected a novation of partnership agreement.)

T.K.M. v. E.H., 844 So.2d 669, FlaApp. 3 Dist., 2003 (April 9, 2003) (Grandparents visitation rights: court retained jurisdiction to enforce mediation agreement expanding visitation rights.)

Wells v. Wells, 832 So.2d 266, Fla.App. 4 Dist., 2002 (Dec. 11, 2002) (Marital Property dispute: provisions of mediation agreement incorporated into divorce judgment against husband were enforceable.)

In re Baron, 283 B.R. 328, Bkrtcy.M.D.Fla., 2002 (May 31, 2002) (Marital Property Settlement nondischargeable: obligations as detailed in mediation agreement and incorporated into final divorce judgment are enforceable.)

Raphael v. Raphael, 817 So.2d 823, La.App. 3 Cir., 2002 (May 8, 2002) (Trusts & Estates issue: court enforced mediation agreement between brothers and sister to partition parents' estate.)

In re Conservatorship of Persona and Estate of Tompkins, 2002 WL 59740, Cal.App. 2 Dist., 2002 (Jan. 17, 2002) (Conservatorship: order in conservatorship proceeding held that mediation agreement between siblings was valid and enforceable, although appealable.)

Baer v. Klagholz, 785 A.2d 907, N.J.Supper.A.D., 2001 (Dec. 29, 2001) (Special Education issues: a mediation agreement is like a settlement agreement enforced thorough a consent decree.)

Forysiak v. Laird Marine and Mfg., 2001 WL 1256402, Ohio App. 6 Dist., 2001 (Oct. 29, 2001) (Service Contract: mediation memorandum of agreement valid as it applied to final settlement agreement.)

Cox v. Hicks, 2001 WL 881356, Tenn. Ct. App., 2001 (Aug. 7, 2001) (Partnership Agreement: mediation agreement regarding property purchase enforceable.)

Hurst v. American Racing Equipment, 981 S.W.2d 458, TexApp.-Texarkana, 1998 (Oct. 16, 1998) (Products Liability: mediation agreement is an enforceable document.)

Vela v. Hope Lumber & Supply Co., 966 P.2d 1196, Okla.Civ.App. Div. 1, 1998 (Automobile negligence: mediation settlement not due to undue influence and coercion, therefore enforceable.)

DeCespedes v. Bolanos, 711 So.2d 216, Fla.App. 3 Dist, 1998 (May 20, 1998) (Dissolution of Company: trial court refused to enforce mediation settlement and opted for judicial dissolution of health care company; appellate court reversed.)

Hermida v. Hermida, 1998 WL 28100, Tex.App.-San Antonio, 1998 (Jan. 28, 1998) (Divorce/Property Settlement: mediation agreement adopted by district court as own judgment.)

Trowbridge v. Trowbridge, 674 So.2d 928, Fla.App. 4 Dist., 1996 (June 12, 1996) (Divorce Settlement: mediation agreement enforceable.)

Island Entertainment, Inc., v. Castaneda, 882 S.W.2d 2, Tex.Appl-Hous. 1 Dist., 1994 (Jan. 20, 1994) (Wrongful Death: mediation agreement valid, but sanctions not appropriate for failure to promptly pay settlement.)

Stempel v. Stempel, 633 So.2d 26, Fla.App. 4 Dist., 1994 (Jan. 19, 1994) (Marriage Dissolution: mediation agreement valid even if details later supplied by court regarding duration of child support and insurance payments.)

Mediation Agreement Not Enforced

Simmons v. Ghaderi, B180735 (Cal.App. 9/27/2006) (Medical malpractice/wrongful death case: cause of action for breach of oral settlement contract; plaintiff estopped from relying on mediation confidentiality statute.)

Dows v. Nike, Inc., 846 So2d 595, Fla.App. 4 Dist., 2003 (May 7, 2003) (Negligence action: no enforceable settlement at time of mediation, subsequent negotiations and final settlement agreement superceded mediation agreement.)

Mills v. Vilas County Bd. Of Adjustments, 660 N.W.2d 705, Wis. App, 2003 (Feb. 6, 2003) (Real Estate seller and Indian tribe: trial court's decision not to enforce mediation agreement based on comity upheld.)

Cloutier v. Cloutier, 814 A.2d 979, Me., 2003 (Jan. 14, 2003) (Marital property dispute: trial court decision that mediated, partial agreement between spouses was not enforceable.)

Georgos v. Jackson, 762 N.E.2d 202, Ind.App., 2002 (Feb. 4, 2002) (Auto accident/insurance settlement: mediation agreement set-aside, plaintiff's attorney present, but not plaintiff, thereby plaintiff suffered as a result of not being party to the discussion.)

Laska v. Laska, 646 N.W.2d 393, Wis.App., 2002 (March 21, 2002) (Probate proceeding: reversal of an order enforcing mediation agreement.)

Hanna v. Schmidt, 707 So.2d 966, Fla.App. 4 Dist., 1998 (April 8, 1998) (Domestic relations/visitation rights: appellate court reversed trial court's enforcement of mediation agreement.)

In re Jason E., 53 Cal.App.4th 1540, CalApp 4 Dist., 1997 (April 2, 1997) (Adoption: based on best interest of the child, court refused to enforce mediation agreement regarding long term guardianship of child between parents, foster parents, and paternal grandparents.)

Snyder-Falkinham v. Stockburger, 1996 WL 1171800, W.D.Va., 1996 (Aug. 5, 1996) (Legal Malpractice action: unsigned mediation agreement not enforceable.)

Feliciano v. Feliciano, 674 So.2d 928, Fla.App. 4 Dist., 1996 (June 12, 1996) (Child Support and Visitation: mediation agreement set aside for best interest of the children.)

Other Issues Related to Enforceability and Confidentiality of Process

Wimsatt v. Superior Court, 61 Cal.Rptr. 3d 200, 152 Cal.App. 4th 125 (2007) (Personal Injury case: mediation briefs submitted to mediator prior to mediation sessions are confidential and cannot be introduced into a court of law as evidence; based on mediation confidentiality statute.)

In re Marriage of Kieturakis, 41 Cal.Rptr.3d 119, 128 Cal.App.4th 56 (2006) (Divorce proceeding: confidentiality of mediation communications is admissible if all participants of mediation waive the prohibition.)

Lehr v. Afflitto, 809 A.2d 462, 382 N.J. Super 376 (2006) (Divorce proceeding: all mediation proceedings including mandatory matrimonial Early Settlement Panel proceedings shall be confidential. Lower court erred in permitting mediator as witness in divorce proceeding.)

Rojas v. Superior Court, 15 Cal.Rptr.3d 642, 33 Cal.4th 407, 93 P.3d 260 (2004) (Landlord/Tenant: mediation confidentiality statue prevails regarding communications.)

Rosewood Services, Inc. v. Sunflower Diversified Services, Inc., 2003 WL 22090897, D.Kan., 2003 (Sept. 8, 2003) (Medicaid Contract Services: mediation agreement did not bar further claims of party.)

Alegria v. Sabo, 2002 WL 32103157. Idaho Dist., 2002 (Nov. 8, 2002) (Sales Contract of restaurant: enforcement of mediation denied due to plaintiff's failure to notice up the motion for hearing.)

Steward v. Hillsboro School Dist. No. 11, 2001 WL 34047100, D.Org., 2001 (March 1, 2001) (Special Education/IDEA: enforcement of mediation agreement through due process proceeding requires all administrative process must be exhausted before filing civil action.)

B.K. v. Toms River Board of Education, 998 F.Supp. 462, D.N.J., 1998 (March 30, 1998) (Special Education/IDEA: plaintiff prevailed on mediation agreement, court unable to determine if attorney fees are inclusive.)

In Matter of Marriage of Allen, 1996 WL 686895, Tex.App.-Amarillo, 1996 (Nov. 27, 1996) (Marital Property: question of whether or not a mediation agreement is enforceable was found moot as neither party asked the trial court to enforce it.)

Tina B. v. Richard T., 1996 WL 913169, OhioApp. 6 Dist., 1996 (May 28, 1996) (Child Support and Vistiation: mediation agreement will become part of enforceable order only if the court has followed all relevant statutory requirements and considered all things required by law, including best interest of the child; appeal dismissed.)

Hudson v. Hudson, 600 So.2d 7, Fla.App. 4 Dist., 1992 (April 29,k 1992) (Divorce: violation of confidentiality of mediation agreement prior to signing vacated judgment and required new trial.)

Regan v. Carriagan, 486 N.W.2d 57, Mich.App., 1992 (Jan. 13, 1992) (Creditor/Debtor issue: conveyance of assets during mediation process invalidates proceedings.)

APPENDIX FOUR

Collaboration Practice Groups

International Academy of Collaborative Professionals; 11811 N. Tatum Blvd, #3031, Phoenix, AZ 85028; www.collaborativepractice. com

Collaborative Dispute Resolution Professionals, Inc. (Montgomery County); http://collablawmaryland.org; PO Box 1262, Rockville, MD 20849; (301) 424-8081

Collaborative Divorce Association (Montgomery County); www. collaborativedivorceMD.com; 25 W. Middle Lane, Rockville, MD 20841; (301) 838-3228

Collaborative Law Society of D.C., Maryland and Virginia (Montgomery County); www.co-divorce.com; 2101 Wilson Blvd, Ste. 950, Arlington, VA 22201; (703) 528-6700

Collaborative Professionals of Southern Maryland, Inc. (Anne Arundel, Prince George's, Calvert, Charles, St. Mary's counties); 7850 Walker Drive, Ste. 160, Greenbelt, MD 20770; (301) 459-8200

Howard County Collaborative Professionals, Inc. (Howard County); www.hococollaborativeprofesionals.com; 10632 Little Patuxent Pkwy, Ste 446, Columbia, MD 21044; (410) 997-0203

Maryland Collaborative Law Association, Inc. (Statewide); www. MarylandCollaborativeLaw.com; 212 W. Main Street, Ste. 208, Salisbury, MD 21801; (410) 749-6118

Maryland Collaborative Practice Council (Statewide); www.marylandcollaborativepractice.com; 25 W. Middle Lane, Rockville, MD 20841; (301) 838-3228

For training opportunities contact: Collaborative Training Solutions, LLC; P.O. Box 424, Eldersburg, MD 21784; (443) 520-9690 or (410) 321-5851

Or

Maryland State Bar Association, Continuing Legal Education, 520 W. Fayette Street, Baltimore, MD 21201; (410) 685-7878; or www. msba.org.

References

Chapter 1

1   C. S. Lewis, "The Lion, the Witch and the Wardrobe" (New York: Collier Books: Macmillan Publishing Co., 1970), 159-60.

2   *International Shoe Co. v. Washington,* 326 U.S. 310, 316 (1945); see also *Burger King Corp. v. Rudzewicz,* 471 U.S. 462, 47 (1985).

3   *Philips Exeter Academy v. Howard Phillips Fund, Inc.,* 196 F.3d 284, 288 (1st Cir. 1999).

4   See 28 U.S.C. § 1332 (2011).

5   *Kramer v. Bally's Park Place, Inc.,* 311 Md. 387, 390, 535 A.2d 466 (1988).

6   *Commercial Union Ins. Co. v. Porter Hayden Co.,* 116 Md.App. 605, 672, 698 A.2d 1167 (1997).

7   *Laboratory Corp. of America v. Hood,* 395 Md. 608, 614, 911 A.2d 841, 844 (2006).

Chapter 2

1   UCC definition of goods.

Chapter 3

1   MD Ann Code Criminal Law §10-603(4)

2   This office regulates horses in Maryland, Delaware, and the District of Columbia for the USDA-APHIS.

3   15USC44 §§ 1821-1831; and for regulations go to 9CFR11.1 et seq.

4   MD Ann Code Agriculture §§2-701 et seq. and COMAR 15.16.01

5   A Coggins test is the official test for equine infectious anemia.

6   COMAR 15.11.01.05

7   COMAR 15.11.12

[8]   MD Ann Code Agriculture §§12-101 et seq.

[9]   Maryland Dept of Agriculture, Equine Show Policies, http:// www.mda. state.md.us/article.php?i=16249

[10]   COMAR 15.11.14.05

[11]   COMAR 15.11.17

[12]   COMAR 15.11.17.02(5)

[13]   A "downer" is any animal that cannot stand and walk without assitance. COMAR 15.11.17.02(2).

[14]   COMAR 15.11.17.04

[15]   MD Ann Code Agriculture §§9-301 thru 9-303

[16]   *See* generally MD Ann Code Agriculture §§108, 110, 111, 113, 116, and 118.

[17]   COMAR 15.11.19

[18]   MD Ann Code Criminal Law §10-604.

Chapter 4

[1]   *Holler v. Lowery,* 175 Md. 149, 157, 200 A. 353, 357 (1938), quoting *"Restatement of Torts" A.L.I.* § 282; see also William L. Prosser, "Handbook of The Law of Torts" § 43, at 250 (4th ed. 1971).

[2]   *Baltimore, C. & A.R. Co. v. Turner,* 152 Md. 216, 228, 136 A. 609, 614 (1927); *Dickey v. Hochschild, Kohn & Co.,* 157 Md. 448, 450, 146 A. 282, 283, (1929); *Schell v. United Rys. & Elec. Co.,* 144 Md. 527, 531, 125 A. 158, 159 (1924).

[3]   *Chicago Title Ins. Co. v. Allfirst Bank,* 394 Md. 270, 290, 905 A.2d 366 (2006); *Valentine v. On Target, Inc.,* 353 Md. 544, 549, 727 A.2d 947 (1999); *Southland Corp. v. Griffith,* 332 Md. 704, 712-13, 633 A.2d 84, 88 (1993); see also Paul Mark Sandler and James K. Archibald, "Pleading Causes of Action in Maryland" §3.28 (MICPEL 4th ed. 2008).

[4]   *Dehn v. Edgecombe,* 384 Md. 606, 619-20, 865 A.2d 603, 611 (2005); *Hemmings v. Pelham Wood,* 375 Md. 522, 536, 826 A.2d 443, 451 (2003).

[5] *McNack v. State*, 398 Md. 378, 395, 920 A.2d 1097, 1107 (2007).

[6] *Montgomery v. Remsburg*, 147 Md. App. 564, 584, 810 A.2d 14, 26 (2002), rev'd and remanded on other grounds, 376 Md. 568, 831 A.2d 18 (2003).

[7] *Paramount*, 249 Md. at 193, 238 A.2d at 871; *Brown*, 236 Md. at 497, 204 A.2d at 531.

[8] W. Page Keeton et al., "Prosser and Keeton on Torts" § 41, at 263 (5th ed.1984); *Stickley v. Chisholm*, 136 Md.App. 305, 314, 765 A.2d 662, 668 (2001); *Murray v. United States*, 215 F.3d 460, 463 (4th Cir. 2000).

[9] *Penn, Steel Company v. Wilkinson*, 107 Md. 574, 69 A. 412 (1908).

[10] *Id.* at 581, 69 A. at 414-415, *quoting* 21 Am. & Eng.Ency. 490.

[11] See *Yonce v. Smith Kline Beecham Clinical Labs., Inc.*, 111 Md.App. 124, 137, 680 A.2d 569 (1996).

[12] *Mayer v. North Arundel Hosp. Ass'n, Inc.*, 145 Md.App. 235, 247, 802 A.2d 483, 490 (2002).

[13] *Bd. of County Comm'rs v. Bell Atlantic-Md.*, 346 Md. 160, 180, 695 A.2d 171, 181 (1997).

[14] *Brady v. Ralph M. Parsons Co.*, 327 Md. 275, 291, 609 A.2d 297, 305 (1992) (quoting RESTATEMENT (SECOND) OF TORTS § 483 (1965)).

[15] *Palenchar v. Jarrett*, 507 F. Supp.2d 502, 512 (D. Md. 2007).

[16] *Pahanish v. Western Trails, Inc.*, 69 Md.App. 342, 357, 517 A.2d 1122 (1986); see also *Slack v. Villari*, 59 Md.App. 462, 470, 476 A.2d 227, cert. denied, 301 Md. 177, 482 A.2d 502 (1984).

[17] *Pahanish*, 69 Md. App. ay 357, 517 A.2d 1122; see also *Finneran v. Wood*, 249 Md. 643, 648, 241 A.2d 579 (1968); *Herbert v. Ziegler*, 216 Md. 212, 216, 139 A.2d 699 (1958); *Twigg v. Ryland*, 62 Md. 380, 386 (1884).

[18] See generally *Ward v. Hartley*, 168 Md. App. 209, 895 A.2d 1111, cert. denied, 394 Md. 310, 905 A.2d 844 (2006) (plaintiff sued landlord in strict liability and negligence when tenant's dog escaped and bit plaintiff).

Chapter 5

1   *See*, e.g., *Lane v. Calvert*, 215 Md. 457, 462, 138 A.2d 902 (1958) (standard of care "such as is ordinarily exercised by others in the profession generally."); *McClees v. Cohen*, 158 Md. 60, 66, 148 A. 124 (1930). *Shofer v. Stuart Hack Co.*, 124 Md. App. 516, 529, 723 A.2d 481 (1999).

2   *See*, e.g., *Walpert, Smullian & Blumenthal, P.A. v. Katz*, 361 Md. 645, 762 A.2d 582 (2000) (accountant malpractice); *Parler & Wobber v. Miles & Stockbridge, P.C.*, 359 Md. 671, 756 A.2d 526 (2000) (legal malpractice); *Dunham v. Elder*, 18 Md. App. 360, 306 A.2d 568 (1973) (medical malpractice).

3   *Kennedy v. Burgess*, 337 Md. 562, 654 A.2d 1335 (1995).

4   Md. Code, *Agriculture Art.* § 2-301, et seq. (2009).

5   *Ferrell v. Benson*, 352 Md. 2, 3, 720 A.2d 583 (1998); see also Susan J. Hankin, "Not a Living Room Sofa: Changing the Legal Status of Companion Animals," 4 Rutgers Journal of Law & Public Policy 321 (Winter 2007); Gary L. Francione, "Introduction: Animals as Property," 2 Animal L., at *2 (1996); Harold W. Hannah, "Animals as Property – Changing Concepts" 25 S. Ill. U. L.J. 571-2 (2001); *Harabes v. Barkery, Inc.*, 791 A.2d 1142, 1144 (N.J. Super. Ct. Law Div. 2001).

6   See MD CODE, Agriculture § 1-101(f).

7   Hankin, 4 Rutgers Journal of Law & Public Policy at 325-27.

8   Md.Code, Cts. & Jud. Proc. § 5-101 (Repl.Vol.1998).

9   *Leonhart v. Atkinson*, 265 Md. 219, 289 A.2d 1 (1972) (malpractice by accountant); *Steelworkers Holding Co. v. Menefee*, 255 Md. 440, 258 A.2d 177 (1969) (malpractice by architect); *Mumford v. Staton, Whaley & Price*, 254 Md. 697, 255 A.2d 359 (1969) (malpractice by attorney); *Mattingly v. Hopkins*, 254 Md. 88, 253 A.2d 904 (1969) (malpractice by civil engineer).

Chapter 6

1   Milton C. Toby & Karen L. Perch, Ph.D., Understanding Equine Law: Your Guide to Horse Health Care and Management, 24 (The Blood-Horse Inc. 1999).

2   MD Ann. Code, Comm Law, Title 2, §2-201(1).

3 MD Ann. Code, Comm Law, Title 16, §16-401.

Chapter 7

1 *Deboy v. Crisfield,* 167 Md. App. 548, 555, 893 A.2d 1189 (2006); *Baltimore Gas & Elec. v. Lane,* 338 Md. 34, 44, 656 A.2d 307 (1995); *Ward v. Hartley,* 168 Md. App. 209, 215, 895 A.2d 1111 (2005); *Rowley v. Mayor,* 305 Md. 456, 464, 505 A.2d 494 (1986); *Rehn v. Westfield America,* 153 Md. App. 586, 592, 837 A.2d 981 (2003); *Doehring v. Wagner,* 80 Md. App. 237, 243, 562 A.2d 762 (1989).

2 *Elmar Gardens, Inc. v. Odell,* 227 Md. 454, 457, 177 A.2d 263 ... (1962); see also *Matthews v. Amberwood Assoc.,* 351 Md. 544, 557, 719 A.2d 119 (1998); *Marshall v. Price,* 162 Md. 687, 689, 161 A. 172 (1932).

3 *Marshall,* 162 Md. at 689, 161 A. 172.

4 *Shields v. Wagman,* 350 Md. 666, 673-74, 714 A.2d 881 (1998); *Macke Laundry Serv. Co. v. Weber,* 267 Md. 426, 435, 298 A.2d 27 (1972); *Windsor v. Goldscheider,* 248 Md. 220, 222, 236 A.2d 16 (1967); *Langley Park Apartments, Sec. H., Inc. v. Lund Adm'r,* 234 Md. 402, 407, 199 A.2d 620 (1964).

5 *Shields,* 350 Md. at 674, 714 A.2d 881 (quoting *Landay v. Cohn,* 220 Md. 24, 27, 150 A.2d 739 (1959)).

6 *Sezzin v. Stark,* 187 Md. 241, 250, 49 A.2d 742 (1946); *Murray v. Lane,* 51 Md.App. 597, 601, 444 A.2d 1069 (1982).

7 *Baltimore Gas & Elec. v. Flippo,* 348 Md. 680, 688, 705 A.2d 1144 (1998) (emphasis added).

8 *Deboy,* 168 Md. App. at 217, 895 A.2d 1111 (quoting *Rowley,* 305 Md. at 465, 505 A.2d 494).

9 *Rivas v. Oxon Hill Joint Venture,* 130 Md. App. 101, 109, 744 A.2d 1076, 1080-1 (2000); *Giant Food v. Mitchell,* 334 Md. 633, 640A.2d 1134 (1994); *McGarr v. Balt. Area Council, Boy Scouts of Am., Inc.,* 74 Md. App. 127, 536 A.2d 728 (1988).

10 *Wells,* 120 Md. App. at 710, 708 A.2d 34; *Howard County Bd. of Educ. v. Cheyne,* 99 Md. App. 150, 155, 636 A.2d 22 (1994).

11 *Wells,* 120 Md. App. at 710, 708 A.2d 34.

[12]   *Id.*

[13]   *State v. Thurston,* 128 Md. App. 656, 661m 739 A.2d 940, 943 (1999).

[14]   *Id.*

[15]   *Id.* at 710-11, 708 A.2d 34.

[16]   *Crown Cork & Seal Co. v. Kane,* 213 Md. 152, 160, 131 A.2d 470 (1957); *Cheyne,* 99 Md. App. at 156, 636 A.2d 22.

[17]   *Kane,* 213 Md. at 160, 131 A.2d 470 (quoting *Kalus v. Bass,* 122 Md. 467, 473, 89 A. 731 (1914)).

[18]   *Bass v. Hardee's Food Sys.,* No. 98-2025, 200 U.S. App. LEXIS 19053, *8 (4th Cir. Aug. 9, 2000).

[19]   *Maans v. Giant of Md., LLC,* 161 Md. App. 620, 871 A.2d 627 (2005); *Univ. of Md. E. Shore v. Rhaney,* 159 Md. App. 44, 53, 858 A.2d 497, 502, *aff'd,* 388 Md. 585, 880 A.2d 357 (2005); *Rivas,* 130 Md. App. at 109, 744 A.2d at 1080-1; *Fenninger v. Harris Crab House, Inc.,* No. 98-2526, 2000 U.S. App. LEXIS 4285, *4-6 (4th Cir. Mar. 20, 2000).

[20]   *State v. Thurston,* 128 Md.App. 656, 661, 739 A.2d 940, 943 (1999) (owner of the horse was a business invitee while exercising his horse at the racetrack adjacent to the Fair Hill training complex)

[21]   *Id.* at 689 (quoting *Lane,* 338 Md. at 44, 656 A.2d 307); see also *Rivas,* 130 Md. App. at 109, 744 A.2d at 1080-1; *Casper v. Chas. F. Smith & Son, Inc.,* 71 Md. App. 445, 526 A.2d 87 (1987), *aff'd,* 316 Md. 573, 560 A.2d 1130 (1989).

[22]   *Wells v. Polland,* 120 Md.App. 699, 710, 708 A.2d 34 (1998).

[23]   *Flippo,* 348 Md. at 689, 705 A.2d 1144 (quoting *Wagner v. Doehring,* 315 Md. 97, 102, 553 A.2d 684 (1989)).

[24]   *Rivas,* 130 Md. App. at 109, 744 A.2d at 1080-1.

[25]   *Flippo,* 348 Md. at 689, 705 A.2d 1144.

[26]   *Id.*

[27]   *Id; Rivas,* 130 Md. App. at 109, 744 A.2d at 1080-1; *Bramble v. Thompson,* 264 Md. 518, 287 A.2d 265 (1972).

[28]   *Rivas,* 130 Md. App. at 109, 744 A.2d at 1080-1; *Flowers v. Rock Creek*

Terrace, 308 Md. 432, 520 A.2d 361 (1987); *Shastri Narayan Swaroop, Inc. v. Hart,* 158 Md. App. 63, 854 A.2d 269 (2004), *aff'd,* 385 Md. 514, 870 A.2d 157 (2005).

29   308 Md. at 447-48, 520 A.2d 361.

30   *Flowers,* 308 Mdd. At 444 n.5, 520 A.2d at 366 n.5.

31   354 Md. at 419-20, 731 A.2d 884 (1999); *see also Rivas,* 130 Md. App. at 109, 744 A.2d at 1080-1.

Chapter 9

1   *Valentine v On Target, Inc.,* 112 Md.App. 679, 686 A2d 636 (Md.App. 1996)

2   Black's Law Dictionary, Bryan A. Garner, 8th Edition, Page 139.

3   *Murphy v BGE, Co.,* 290 Md. 186, 428 A2d 459 (Md. 1981)

4   West's Ann.Md.Code, Natural Resources, § 5-1101 et. seq.

5   *See Fagerhus v. Host Marriott, Corp.,* 2002, 795 A.2d 221, 143 Md. App. 525, *certiorari denied* 801 A.2d 1032, 369 Md. 572 (Recreational use statute, generally relieving owner of land from duty to keep premises safe for entry or use by others for any recreational or educational purpose, covers all "non-paying" recreational and educational users, without regard to how such users might otherwise be categorized under common law.)

6   Jonathan S. Kayes, Extension Specialist – Natural Resources, Univ. of MD Cooperative Extension, Landowner Liability and Recreational Access Extension Bulletin #357 (Revised June 2008)

7   James Clark-Dawe, Esquire, "Equine Liability – What Every Horse Owner Needs to Know," 166 (Carriage House Publishing 2003).

8   Terence J. Centner, The New Equine Liaiblity Statues, 62 Tenn. L. Rev. 997, 1001 (1995).

9   Kathleen J.P. Tabor, Esquire, "Mediation and Arbitration Clauses in Equine Contracts (The importance of resolving conflicts while maintaining mutually beneficial relationships)," Entertainment and Sports Lawyer, Vol. 22, No. 3, Fall 2004.

10   MD Dept of Agriculture, County Agricultural and Land Use Information,

http://www.mda.state.md.us/on_web/ag_links/countyag.php, accessed August 20, 2010

[11]   MD Dept. of Natural Resources, Maryland Environmental Trusts, http://www.dnr.state.md.us/met/ce.html, accessed August 20, 2010

[12]   Maryland Agricultural Land Preservation Foundation, http://www.malpf.info/, accessed August 20, 2010

Chapter 10

[1]   Treas. Regs. § 1.83-2(b)(1).

[2]   Treas. Regs. § 1.83-2(b)(2).

[3]   Treas. Regs.§ 1.83-2(b)(3).

[4]   Treas. Regs. § 1.83-2(b)(4), see also *Purdue v. Commissioner*, 922 F.2d 833 (3rd Cir. 1993); *LaMusga v. Commissioner*, T.C. Memo. 1987-742; Estate of Margaret Love, T.C. Memo. 198-470.

[5]   Treas. Regs. § 1.83-2(b)(5).

[6]   Treas. Regs. § 1.83-2(b)(6), see also *Keller v. Commissioner*, 95-1 USTC ¶ 50,250 (6th Cir. 1995).

[7]   Treas. Regs. § 1.83-2(b)(7).

[8]   Treas. Regs. § 1.83-2(b)(8).

[9]   Treas. Regs. § 1.83-2(b)(9).

[10]   Thomas A. Davis, "2006 Horse Owners and Breeders Tax Handbook" (American Horse Council 2005), § 1.03(a) at page 1-8.

[11]   IRC § 162(a).

[12]   Davis, §4.01 at 4-2.

[13]   In applicable part, Section 8-209 of the Tax-Property Article of the Annotated Code of Maryland provides:

(a) The General Assembly declares that it is in the general public interest of the State to foster and encourage farming activities to:

(1) maintain a readily available source of food and dairy products

close to the metropolitan areas of the State:

(2) encourage the preservation of open space as an amenity necessary for human welfare and happiness; and

(3) prevent the forced conversion of open space land to more intensive uses because of the economic pressures caused by the assessment of the land at rates or levels incompatible with its practical use for farming.

(b) It is the intention of the General Assembly that the assessment of farmland:

(1) be maintained at levels compatible with the continued use of the land for farming; and

(2) not be affected adversely by neighboring land uses of a more intensive nature."

While these provisions establish the overall philosophy for the agricultural use assessment program, the law also includes:

(a) Specific provisions relating to the criteria to be used in determining whether or not lands qualify for the agricultural use assessment.

(b) Tests to be considered by the assessors.

(c) Situations where the use assessment cannot apply.

(d) Application of the agricultural use assessment to woodland

[14] Maryland SDAT website at www.dat.state.md.us/sdateweb/agtransf.html

Chapter 11

[1] Julie I. Fershtman, "Equine Law and Horse Sense," p. 27 (Horses & The Law Publishing 1996).

[2] *Nationwide Mutual Insurance Company v. Darden,* 503 U.S. 318, 322-23 (1992) (quoting *Community for Creative Non-Violence v. Reid,* 490 U.S. 730, 739-740, 109 S.Ct. 2166, 2172, 104 L.Ed.2d 811 (1989).

[3] *Id.* at 323-24 (quoting *Community for Creative Non-Violence v. Reid,* 490 U.S. 730, 751-52 (1989)). *See also Mangram v. General Motors Corp.,* 108 F.3d 61 (4th Cir.1997) (applying common law factors in determining whether claimant under ADEA is employee); *Robb v. United States,* 80 F.3d 884 (4th Cir.1996) (applying common law principles to determine

federal question of whether physician was independent contractor for purposes of FTCA); *cf. Garrett v. Phillips Mills, Inc.,* 721 F.2d 979 (4th Cir.1983) (applying similar 12-factor test to determine whether claimant under ADEA is an employee); *Haavistola v. Community Fire Co. of Rising Sun,* 6 F.3d 211 (4th Cir.1993) (applying *Garrett* factors in Title VII case).

4 *Farlow v. Wachovia Bank of N.C., N.A.,* 259 F.3d 309, 314 (4th Cir.2001) (holding that an attorney working for a bank was an independent contractor because she did not receive benefits or a regular paycheck and was treated like a contractor and in spite of the fact that she was required to attend staff meetings and hold bank-specified office hours, and that the bank supplied her with a company car, computer, office, and administrative assistant).

5 *Id.* at 315.

6 *Id.* at 315.

7 *Secretary of Labor, U.S. Dept. of Labor v. Lauritzen,* 835 F.2d 1529, 1534 (7th Cir.1987). The FLSA defines an "employee" as "any individual employed by an employer." id.§ 203(e)(1). An employer includes "any person acting directly or indirectly in the interest of an employer in relation to an employee." 29 U.S.C. § 203(d). The FLSA "defines the verb 'employ' expansively to mean 'suffer or permit to work.' " 29 U.S.C. § 203(g); *see also Nationwide Mut. Ins. Co. v. Darden,* 503 U.S. 318, (1992). These definitions broaden "the meaning of 'employee' to cover some workers who might not qualify as such under more traditional agency or contract law principles." Id.

8 *Henderson v. Inter-Chem Coal Co.,* 41 F.3d 567, 570 (10th Cir.1994) (citing *Bartels v. Birmingham,* 332 U.S. 126 (1947)).

9 *Id.; see also Martin v. Selker Bros., Inc.,* 949 F.2d 1286, 1293 (3d Cir.1991); *Brock v. Superior Care, Inc.,* 840 F.2d 1054, 1059 (2d Cir.1988); *Usery v. Pilgrim Equip. Co.,* 527 F.2d 1308, 1311 (5th Cir.1976).

10 *Herman v. Mid-Atlantic Installation Servs., Inc.,* 164 F.Supp.2d 667, 671 (D. Md. 2000).

11 *Henderson,* 41 F.3d at 570.

12 *Steelman v. Hirsch,* 473 F.3d 124, 129 (4th Cir. 2007).

13 26 U.S.C. § 3121(d).

14 *See* 26 C.F.R. § 31.3121(d)-1 ("Who are employees"); id. § 31.3121(d)-2

("Who are employers"), and official IRS interpretations set out 20 factors to be considered in making that determination, *see* IRS Rev. Rul. 87-41; 26 C.F.R. §§ 31.3306(i)-1, 31.3401(c)-1.

[15] *Weber v. C.I.R.,* 60 F.3d 1104, 1111 (4th Cir. 1995).

[16] *Id.*

[17] *Sanders v. Rowan,* 61 Md.App. 40, 51, 484 A.2d 1023 (1984).

[18] *See Sawyer v. Humphries,* 322 Md. 247, 587 A.2d 467 (1991).

[19] *Bell v. State,* 153 Md. 333, 340, 138 A. 227, 58 A.L.R. 1051.

[20] *B. P. Oil Corp. v. Mabe,* 279 Md. 632, 370 A.2d 554 (1977); *Sun Cab Co. v. Powell,* 196 Md. 572, 577-78, 77 A.2d 783 (1951); *Keitz v. National Paving and Contracting Co.,* 214 Md. 479, 491, 134 A.2d 296 (1957).

[21] *Id.* (quoting Restatement of Agency 2d, § 2(1)).

[22] *Id.* at 255, 587 A.2d at 470-71.

[23] *Id.* (quoting *Hopkins C. Co. v. Read Drug & C. Co.,* 124 Md. 210, 214, 92 A. 478, 479-80 (1914)).

[24] *See id.* at 255, 587 A.2d at 471.

[25] *See id.* at 256-57, 587 A.2d at 471.

[26] *Id.* at 257, 587 A.2d at 471.

Chapter 12

[1] MD Rules of Procedure, 17-102(a)

[2] Title 17, The Maryland Rules

[3] One who represents oneself in a court proceeding without the assistance of a lawyer. (Black's Law Dictionary, 8th Edition), Page 1258.

[4] Black's Law Dictionary, 8th Edition, Page 1003.

[5] *Warner v. Lerner,* 348 Md. 733, 705 A.2d 1169, 1171 (1998).

[6] Maryland Rules of Procedure 17-102 (2003).

[7] *County Commissioners of Caroline County v. J. Roland Dashiell & Sons, Inc.,*

358 Md. 83, 747 A.2d 600, 606 (2000).

8 Maryland Rules of Procedure 17-102(h) (2003)

9 Maryland Rules of Procedure 17-102(b) (2003)

10 International Academy of Collaborative Professionals, Protocols of Practice for Civil Collaborative Lawyers. The protocols are to be used on a voluntary basis as a guideline, by lawyers who are trained in the collaborative process. www.collaborativepractice.com.

11 "Being or involving uncompensated legal services performed esp. for the public good." Black's Law Dictionary, 8th Edition, Page 1240.

Chapter 13

1 Kathleen Tabor, "Benefits and Liabilities of (the) Equine Industry," Maryland Bar Journal, Sept. 2007

2 *Id.*

3 "Is Your Hobby a For-Profit Endeavor?", FS-2008-23, June 2008, http://www.irs.gov/irs/article/0,,id=186056,00.html, accessed August 23, 2010

4 *Id.*

5 26CFR1.183-1

6 Richard W. Craigo, Esq. and Paul B. Husband, Esq.,"An Ounce of Prevention: Gaining the Upper Hand Over the IRS," University of Kentucky College of Law, Office of Continuing Legal Education, 23rd Annual National Conference on Equine Law, April 30 & May 1, 2008, Lexington, KY.

7 *Id.*

Chapter 14

1 Data released February 8, 2011, 2010 Maryland Equine Census (USDA-NASS)

Sample Forms

[1] Note to Drafter: check appropriate title under MD CORP & ASSNS § 1-101 et seq. and note specific title in this section. Title 2, Maryland Corporations; Title 4A, Maryland Limited Liability Act; Title 5, Special Types of Corporations; Title 9, Uniform Partnership Act; Title 10, Limited Partnership Act; Title 12, Business Trusts.

[2] Note to Drafter: Non-profits, or Tax-Exempt Non-Stock Corporations, file Articles of Incorporation and would use "Bylaws" rather than an "Operating Agreement" as its operational document. Limited Liability Partnerships file a Certificate of Limited Liability Partnership.

[3] Hypothecation is the pledging of something as security without delivery of title or possession.

[4] NOTE: Articles of Cancellation are filed for LLCs; Articles of Dissolution are filed for all other Maryland corporations.